ECOLOGY AND THE CRISIS OF OVERPOPULATION

Sneh – for taking an interest

Ecology and the Crisis of Overpopulation

Future Prospects for Global Sustainability

Anup Shah

Lecturer in Economics,
University of Newcastle upon Tyne, UK

Edward Elgar

Cheltenham, UK • Northampton, MA, USA

Published by
Edward Elgar Publishing Limited
Glensanda House
Montpellier Parade
Cheltenham
Glos GL50 1UA
UK

Edward Elgar Publishing, Inc.
6 Market Street
Northampton
Massachusetts 01060
USA

A catalogue record for this book is available from the British Library

Library of Congress Cataloguing in Publication Data
Shah, Anup.
    Ecology and the crisis of overpopulation: future prospects for
global sustainability/Anup Shah.
    Includes bibliographical references and index.
    1. Population—Environmental aspects. 2. Demographic transition.
3. Overpopulation. 4. Economic development—Environmental aspects.
I. Title.
HB849.415.S5   1998
304.2'8—dc21   98–21064
                                                    CIP

ISBN 1 85898 463 7

Printed and bound in Great Britain by Bookcraft (Bath) Ltd.

Contents

Figures and table

Preface

The widespread concern with the earth's natural environment persists. The main interest appears to be focused on the impact of human activity on both the quantity and the quality of the world's biomass. One of the driving forces behind the rapid increase in human economic activity is human population growth. Therefore, it should be interesting to examine what economists have to say on this subject. But it also turns out that behavioural ecologists have uncovered some interesting insights concerning population size and change in natural environments. It therefore appears worth taking a closer look at a possible synthesis between the two disciplines.

Accordingly, this book attempts to explain the world population phenomenon and its global consequences by blending the insights of analytical economics and behavioural ecology. The book is more concerned with building an overall picture than filling in the details of the picture since, in a task such as this, it appears that priority is best given to explaining the stylized facts. In constructing the broad picture, many technicalities have been replaced with verbal logic. Notwithstanding the importance of details and techniques, the primary aim is that the reader should be able to grasp the main arguments with minimal fuss.

Given the scope of the subject matter, the book should appeal to all economists and other social scientists, geographers, earth scientists, ecologists, biologists and zoologists who are interested in the topic of population and the environment. Those engaged in teaching multi-disciplinary courses at institutions of higher education may find it useful. It should also be suitable for students undertaking post-graduate work across disciplines as well as more advanced researchers who delight in thinking through novel ideas. In addition, policy makers in governments, non-government organizations (NGO) and international institutions should find the book both accessible and thought-provoking.

Finally, it is worth stating that although the book attempts to answer some awkward questions about human population size and growth, it is written in the knowledge that the more difficult task is to take on board novel and possibly uncomfortable ideas with a view to formulating the somewhat unpalatable questions themselves.

1 Introduction

1.1 The population problem

Trends

Suppose we observe the earth at two different points in time, the present and the past. Presently, we observe islands of the natural environment surrounded by us and our artefacts whereas in the past we would have observed pockets of humanity surrounded by the natural environment. Interestingly, 10000 years ago there were only four million of us. Had our brains not developed and had we not learnt technology then agriculture would not have happened and, in all probability, our population would have stayed at four million. Of course, agriculture did happen and we transformed vast areas of the natural environment into grazing land and crop land. We did not stop at agriculture; we mined minerals, prospected for oil and coal, built urban areas, and laid down highways and railways. Inevitably, in carrying out such a transformation, we lost both quantity and quality of natural environment.

The outcome has been that the earth currently supports 5.8 billion humans with some of us living in great prosperity. Many of us also live healthier lives and longevity has increased. Furthermore, great advances have been made in our stock of knowledge and in our creative endeavours. Such achievements are awesome (Simon, 1996). So what is the problem?

The problem arises from the implication of the prediction that the world population is expected to stabilize at double the present number in about sixty years time. If so, then we could easily lose more of the natural environment (see Ehrlich and Ehrlich, 1992). What seems to worry some observers is that even at today's population size the world's environmental resources are being depleted at a rate faster than at any time in the past. Therefore, they cannot believe that about 12 billion people can be fed without doing irreversible damage to the environment. Why irreversible? Ecologists are reaching a consensus that the natural environment is fast becoming less resilient and that we are reaching a limit which, if breached, may destroy the resilience. A doubling of world population could easily do that.

That there is a serious environmental implication is by no means a universal view. There is a school of thought that believes that increasing the stock of human beings boosts human capabilities and achievements (see Wattenberg and Zinsmeister, 1986, Simon, 1981 and Simon and Kahn, 1984). However, it ignores the role played by the environment in our accomplishments. Even if this school is persuaded to accept the possibility that human ingenuity and the natural environment are complementary inputs in the production of technological and other achievements, it still believes that either technology will be invented such that environmental damage can be minimized in the future or that new technology will enable us to abandon planet Earth and live elsewhere in the solar system.

A welfare problem

Undoubtedly feeding 12 billion people may be an achievement of a sort. However, it raises the hackles of a welfare economist. For such an analyst, what matters is attaining the highest possible level of welfare and so the question arises: can we do better than feeding 12 billion people? In terms of another question, what is the optimum population size? Surprisingly, this question has rarely been addressed. (An exception is the Green Party which boldly states that Britain's optimum population size is 20 million, one-third of the current population.)

What goes into defining optimum population is not only the material standard of living but also the quality of life in which the natural environment, an absence of overcrowding, freedom or minimal regulations, absence of squalor, absence of infectious disease, and so on all figure. These dimensions of quality of life are 'public' in nature which suggests that if 'overpopulation' is behind these external effects, then the collective outcome of private family size decision-making needs to be closely examined. If we find that there are, indeed, welfare-reducing external effects arising from private decision-making then can we devise social institutions to minimize these externalities? Compared to our record in technological invention and innovation, our record of creating effective social institutions is patchy. Clearly, there is scope for achievement here.

1.2   Methodology

This monograph begins by looking at our past. Our past is characterized by frequent changes. It is doubtful if we ever experienced any period of equilibrium. The future, too, may turn out to be characterized by repeated shocks. Given this scenario, how can an economist contribute to knowledge?

We can draw an analogy with the subject of meteorology. The weather never settles down. It never repeats itself exactly. It is essentially unpredictable a fortnight or so in advance. And yet we can comprehend and explain almost everything that we see up there. We can identify important features such as weather fronts, jet streams, and high-pressure systems. We can understand their dynamics. We can understand how they interact to produce weather on a local and regional scale. In short, we have a real science of weather but without full prediction.

Accordingly, the stance taken in this monograph is that the essence of inquiry is comprehension and explanation. Population growth is viewed as a dynamic social and ecological phenomenon that we can try to understand and explain.

In fact, we shall concentrate on explaining two puzzling observations: our phenomenally rapid growth and our tendency to overcrowd or go beyond optimum population size.

1.3 The nature of the analysis

Decision-making at the household level
An explanation for population size and dynamics could usefully start with the decision-making of a breeding couple. Given that procreation is a biological activity, it would be inadvisable to ignore biological influences on such decision-making.

Accordingly, the monograph begins by going back in time to the age when biological influences were paramount. We shall argue that our ancestors lived in a natural environment that was subject to frequent shocks so that the family size decision-making took the form of a gamble.

The strand of such micro-economic decision-making runs through each of the early chapters, the basic model being updated to incorporate human development in rational thinking. Thus we eventually arrive at the decision-making of the modern western couple where the model is the familiar one of utility maximization subject to a resource constraint. In addition, the decision-making is carried out under less uncertainty than in the past. In today's third world, however, economic survival is highly uncertain and a couple has a more limited access to resources. To this extent, a modified micro-model is also worked out in order to analyse the third world population phenomenon.

Two distinct schools of thought emerge from analyses of the micro models. One is the neo-Malthusian and the other is mainstream economics. There are stark differences between the two schools. One difference is in the terms of trade between parental consumption and children. The schools respond with very different answers to the following question posed to parents: how much bribe would you take in order to not have the marginal child?

Collective consequences
It is the collective consequences of such private decision-making that are particularly interesting and they are analysed at the appropriate places in these earlier chapters. The collective consequences tell us whether or not private decision-making is consistent with social welfare and so this part of the monograph's analysis can have policy implications. As noted above, in pursuing their family size objectives, each couple will aim for the private optimum family size but the collective outcome may be socially sub-optimum. The reason may be adverse externalities which households directly inflict on each other and indirectly when they compete for the natural and other resources to support their families. Unsurprisingly, both neo-Malthusians and mainstream

economists differ in their predictions of the collective consequences. Incidentally, another vital difference between the two schools can be seen in terms of causality between population and poverty; the neo-Malthusians think that population causes poverty whereas the mainstream economists think the other way round. This means that the former school thinks poverty is voluntary whereas the latter believes it is involuntary.

Finally, the policy implications are vastly different. For example, neo-Malthusians claim that the use of contraceptives increases family sizes whereas mainstream economists think that contraceptives help reduce family sizes.

1.4 The plan of this monograph

This monograph is organized in four parts. Part 1 consists of Chapters 2 and 3 and analyses a long sweep of our human history. Such a start to the monograph is essential since population is a long-term phenomenon which has been influenced by some fundamental changes in our history. And, of course, we have always been making family size decisions.

If we go sufficiently far back in our history, as we do in Chapter 2, then it is reasonable to assume that family size decisions were largely influenced by genetic imperatives. However, our ancestors were also capable of rational thought. They also had to learn and adjust given the great uncertainty concerning child survival. Therefore, it is likely that they had a fairly sophisticated breeding strategy in the form of a gamble and this gamble makes up the analytical core of Chapter 2.

Such gambles are bound to be influenced by changes in constraints facing a couple and one change of major significance – in fact, arguably the most momentous change in our entire history – occurred about 10000 years ago. Behavioural ecologists think that it is this that explains the truly astonishing feature of population economics, the exponential population growth curve. Chapter 3, accordingly, brings out the causal link between the former and the latter.

While the analysis of Part 1 is ecological, that of Part 2, consisting of Chapters 4–6 is economic. The transition in the analysis is smoothly accomplished by focusing on Malthusian economics. Malthus was largely responsible for making population economics based on ecological foundations a subject of serious study but in the nineteenth and the first eight decades of the twentieth century he was largely ignored. The reason was that his pessimistic predictions failed to materialize. With hindsight, it appears that despite his sound ecological logic, his analysis was based on inaccurate medium-run assumptions.

As a consequence, the modern micro-economic theory of family size decision-making (Chapter 5) is couched in the familiar language of household utility maximization subject to a budget constraint. Interestingly, although both the ecological and the economic models produce vastly different results, they can be combined in the single framework presented in Chapter 5.

Breeding strategies will, of course, vary with the constraints and these are primarily shaped by the environment. For example, a third world couple faces a great deal of survival uncertainty (Chapter 6). In addition, the couple is typically poor with meagre assets. These characteristics affect its decision-making in a markedly different way from that of the first world couple even if we ignore any cultural differences between the two. The gamble taken by the third world couple is particularly important since the bulk of the world population growth is expected to take place in the third world.

Part 3, comprising chapters 7–10, is normative analysis. It builds on micro decision-making to consider the collective consequences of the given micro behaviour. If the collective outcome of individual behaviour coincides with maximum social welfare then we could say that there is no social welfare problem. If it doesn't then we can either have a non-zero game situation in which social welfare can be raised by raising everyone's welfare, the trick being an elimination of inefficiencies, or a zero sum game situation in which social welfare is raisable but there are individual winners and losers.

There are strong reasons to think that individual behaviour is out of line with social optimum. Most of them have to do with external effects that arise from individual behaviour and Chapter 7 contains an in-depth look at the more important externalities. The analytical point made there is this: because of incorrect pricing, especially of environmental goods, individual behaviour is 'excessive' in such a way that everyone's behaviour adversely affects everyone else's.

Chapter 8 is a justification for the policy of Chapters 9 and 10 that follow. A justification for intervention is needed because our record of social and economic intervention is poor. Since our record of technological progress is excellent, there is the temptation to shirk institutional intervention in population matters and let technological progress take care of problems of poverty and, hopefully, population. On the other hand, the effects of technical progress take time to spread and are uncertain whereas population problems are serious and persistent.

Policy: to intervene or not?
All this is elaborated upon in Chapter 8. Here we digress on the more general remarks concerning the question: to intervene or not?

There may be a case for intervention when markets fail and so give rise to a population problem. For example, when the prices of environmental goods like firewood, fodder and so on are 'too low' the cost of child rearing is also 'too small', giving each third world rural couple a strong private incentive to have a large family.

Before advocating active intervention, it is worth checking out the following: (a) to what extent are markets responsible for large families and (b) can intervention put any market failure right? Consider (a) first. Although the price of environmental goods may be 'too low', the market may find other ways of mitigating the resultant tendency to have large families. Turning to (b) it is not obvious that governments can do something about large families simply because of their poor record of intervention. It may be the case that government intervention in the past has gone against the desires and aspirations of the people and this, in the long run, spells policy failure. Governments may have done such because of asymmetric information concerning people's preferences. It is also not obvious that governments have other information which is superior to that of the market.

The case for intervention really rests on the government being in the business of identifying collective problems resulting from private actions and having the means (resources, planning networks, altruistic politicians and skilled bureaucrats) to solve them. Population and environmental problems are prime candidates for intervention because these problems appear to result from the collective consequences of private actions, have persisted and, indeed, got worse.

However, as mentioned, there are limits to intervention. It does not work against the desires, wishes and aspirations of the people. Then there is the problem of finding out about the appropriate incentives: in the case of family size, to which incentives, ecological or economic, do couples largely respond? There is also the practical problem of motivating people, for example, persuading them to overcome inertia. Finally, there is uncertainty: it is only with hindsight that we recognize the correct policy that should have been carried out. The problem of foresight becomes acute in a real world that is subjected to many and frequent shocks.

There is also an interesting moral issue behind intervention. To elaborate, consider population growth to which there are three impetuses: high birth rates, people living longer and falling child mortality. Therefore, population growth can be cut by reducing birth rates, by encouraging euthanasia, and by reducing health care. Of these three measures, there is a consensus that the first is the most preferred. The moral principle appears to be that to kill something living is highly undesirable. This principle is embraced by most mainstream economists who think that if by restricting population policy in this way the resulting population growth is 'excessive' then we should look for mechanisms to raise prosperity and thereby compensate the living for this 'excess'. However, neo-Malthusians think that it is more important to get the population growth rate right and if abortion and euthanasia are necessary to accomplish that goal then it is a price well worth paying.

Returning to the plan of Chapter 8, its second half deals with the solution to the family size problem by analysing self-regulation at the community level. Self-regulation is an alternative to direct intervention and its commendable feature is that it is usually arrived at by consensus. Therefore, it is thought to have the best chance of working over the long term. However, for self-regulation to work with success, the right conditions need to be in place and Chapter 8 examines such conditions.

It is, of course, an empirical question whether conditions for successful self-regulation exist in reality. If they do not, then we have to look at policy alternatives. Accordingly, Chapter 9 considers a policy in favour with mainstream economists. Labelled as 'win-win' because it reduces both poverty and population growth, the policy is based on the experiences of countries in Western Europe, and more recently, the South East Asian economies. Although there are differences of detail in the experiences of the various countries, the broad sequence of events has been: an industrialization driven increase in prosperity followed, with a sizeable time lag, by a reduction in fertility. The 'win-win' policy is attractive but faces two awkward questions: one is the considerable delay involved in fertility decline and the other is the environmental constraint: is it really feasible for every country to become prosperous by industrializing? Imagine if India and China were to go for 'win-win' policy.

It is sobering to think, perhaps due to the two reasons given above, that in the past these two population giants decided to reduce population growth by more direct intervention. Their policies were in line with neo-Malthusian thinking and their experiences are analysed in the first half of Chapter 10. Since their experiences have met with mixed success, the second half of the chapter explores a policy that combines the best of 'win-win' and neo-Malthusian policies which should be an improvement. The idea is to raise prosperity but, at the same time, reduce fertility fast. Any problems, particularly of the practical kind, arising from such a policy are also prised out in this chapter.

Turning to the final Part, Chapter 11 looks at the urban future. If, despite population control policies and the environment permitting, world population continues both to grow and drift to the urban areas, then the future of the world looks like being highly urban. We can also expect a marked contrast between the affluence of the first world cities and the poverty of the third world cities. This picture of the future living arrangements is simply an extension of the ongoing transformation of the natural environment with which we began this Introduction. Therein lies the most intriguing question of all: what is the optimum amount of the natural environment? Its answer overlaps with the answer to the question of the optimum population.

This monograph concludes with Chapter 12. First, the population problem is restated and then the logic of the entire monograph is presented as a 50-step argument. Finally, all the recurrent themes of the monograph are collected and presented from a novel perspective.

PART I

ECOLOGICAL ANALYSIS

2 The ecological foundations of fertility

2.1 Introduction

Copulation is one of our most successful behavioural patterns – there are nearly six billion human beings alive today to testify to this. In stark contrast, there were only four million of us 10000 years ago, an extremely short period in terms of evolutionary time.

It should therefore come as no surprise that this chapter is about breeding strategies or family size decisions. Paradoxically, given the human characteristics of insatiable sexual appetite and no breeding season, family size decisions imply some sort of birth control. More precisely, the topic of this chapter is about the origins of private birth control. Such origins must have had strong biological influences given that procreation is a biological act and that modern civilization is a recent phenomenon.

It also appears that the family size decision, as analysed in this chapter, has an economic dimension. Simply stated, each family has a motive/objective but each family also faces a resource constraint. This, of course, is the familiar micro-economic problem. The twist is that whereas the resource constraint is economic, the objective is entirely biological and therefore new to economists. (The modern economist should find Chapter 4, which treads familiar grounds, more reassuring.)

This chapter covers human experience over a long period in our distant past: 100000 BC to 10000 BC. Surprisingly, this period was one of remarkable stability – population size did not change a great deal. By covering a long period of stability this chapter also lays down the fundamental groundwork to enable us later on to tackle two basic questions: one, to what extent has our breeding motive changed (not for the five per cent of the affluent but for the 95 per cent of the poor)? Second – since the motive needs to be analysed in relation to constraints – to what extent has the resource constraint facing a given household changed?

This chapter also sets the stage for the expansion of human population, from four million 10000 years ago to nearly six billion today. It is indeed surprising to learn that the earth was sparsely populated in the past (McEvedy and Jones, 1979). Given that 10000 years ago there were no urban areas and technology was extremely primitive, it is once again appropriate to seek an ecological explanation for this observation of a thinly populated earth.

2.2   Early humans

Pelvic bone development

About a million years ago, according to one theory, a change of fundamental importance took place. Due to a chance mutation, some of the ground-living apes were born with a different kind of pelvis (see Bateson, 1988, who also argues that behaviour change precedes anatomical change). Most likely this type of mutation also occurred among the tree-living apes but up there it had no evolutionary advantage (see Lewis, 1960). On the ground, however, it was a different matter because this change in pelvis meant that the ape had to walk upright on two legs. For the first time the upper limbs were free and thus tools could be carried in the hands. With the aid of tools these upright apes gained a survival advantage over their relatives on all fours and thus the mutation survived.

The human brain develops

We had human bodies before we had human intelligence. We were walking while the brain was still that of an ape. But with the arrival of the upright stance, a premium was now placed on brain rather than muscle and those humans who, by chance mutation, developed better brains and were therefore better tool-users, were selected again and again. The brain thus evolved, reaching its present highly developed stage.

Humans as pack hunters

The traditional view is that our ancestors left the forests to hunt large prey animals (see, Ardrey, 1967). It is not clear how it happened but we ended up as pack-hunters. The important implication is that we learnt co-operation. Our ancestors had to help each other in order to hunt successfully. It is likely that later on mutual aid and group cohesion developed from this initial lesson in co-operation and that the urge to co-operate in the modern humans can be traced to this beginning (Lee and De Vore, 1968). Later on in this monograph we shall see how co-operation can, in theory, overcome modern population problems.

With group hunting occurred a new development. Co-operative hunting of large prey put females with babies at risk. They, together with the old and the disabled, had to be left somewhere safe. It also had to be a base to which the hunting males could return. In order to make the fixed base safe, protection had to be erected and so homes came to be built. Equally important, our ancestors began learning territoriality. Later on we shall see how population size and territories relate.

Alongside territoriality, another significant development was that of division of labour. While women stayed behind in the caves or huts at the home base, men organized hunts to kill big game. Over time, the division of labour became greater as women specialized as food-gatherers whereas men became even more efficient at hunting, a feature which is echoed in many of today's indigenous communities. The hunters were also quite capable of using great intelligence to lay down strategies for hunting. They had another advantage: the availability of primitive weapons such as a spear with a stone point. The advantages of intelligence and weapons were indispensable since humans have puny bodies, weak teeth and no claws (Mellars and Stringer, 1989).

Humans spread all over the earth
One consequence of our changing from fruit-picking forest dwellers to meat-eating savanna hunters was that we had leisure time; one large meal of meat lasts a long time. With leisure at hand, we were able to develop aspects of social life. Then, after we learnt to cook and dry our meat, we also discovered that it could be carried with us. Moreover, the skins and furs of killed animals could be used to keep our bodies warm. With our growing brain resulting from natural selection – that is, chance mutation increased brain size which increased survival chances of those with larger brains – we were able to invent more complex tools and devices such as bows and arrows for hunting and bridges and boats for crossing rivers. As a result of these developments we were able to range further. So, as our population increased, there was an absence of any overpopulation problem since the more adventurous moved out into unexplored regions (Foley, 1987). Some 50 000 years ago humans were found only in the tropics and warmer belts of the Old World. Northern Europe was reached 30 000 years ago, then Siberia 20 000 years ago and the Americas 11 000 years ago. As a consequence, throughout the Earth, there were pockets of human population (Gamble, 1994).

2.3   Family size decisions
The above brief sketch of early human history provides us with the context in which to analyse the key question of this chapter: how does a household determine the number of young?

Breeding motive
According to ecologists, there is one motive for procreation: to leave behind the maximum number of surviving children who are capable of reproducing in turn. Since children are the vehicle for passing on one's genes, the basic motive boils down to reproduce so as to pass on genes into eternity; hereditary immortality, in other words. Indeed, some biologists (Dawkins, 1989) think that the preservation and replication of one's genes is the ultimate rationale for one's existence. We can then say that the preferences of a person are such that he/she wants the maximum number of surviving children.

Breeding strategies
Ecologists call family size decisions breeding strategies. They are shaped by the twin realizations that the eventual outcome of breeding is uncertain and that

resources to bear and rear children are limited. Two polar gambits can be distinguished – the small egg gambit and the large young gambit (Colinvaux, 1976). The rationale behind each type is easy to understand: a trade-off between number and egg size, given limited resources, and the fact that survival chances may be increased either by having more babies or by having stronger babies.

The small egg gambit (quantity-biased strategy)

This gambit is associated with species such as houseflies, mosquitoes, salmon and dandelions in which thousands of tiny eggs or seeds are produced. There is a vast range of eventualities that can cause the death of an egg so each egg has a very tiny chance of surviving. To cover the high risk of death faced by each egg it makes sense to have many eggs. However, resources are limited so that parents have to get the balance between egg strength and the numbers right. The housefly that lays too many eggs risks weak eggs and hence jeopardizes survival chances. The housefly that lays too few eggs also risks punishment of fewer survivors and a greater probability of hereditary oblivion. The small egg gambit is similar to the casino gambler's strategy of covering every number with a low-value chip.

The large young gambit (quality-biased strategy)

In the small egg gambit each one of the tiny eggs is at a high risk of death and so, to compensate, many eggs are laid. Alternatively, an animal could produce larger and therefore stronger eggs, but fewer in number given that there is limited parental capital to work with. However, each egg should have a lower risk of death. This is the large young gambit; compared with fish that follow the small egg gambit, animals go for the large young gambit.

Consider birds: in the large young gambit, where each offspring that hatches is cared for until it is able to reproduce, the idea is to get at the optimum clutch size (call this private family planning). Too many eggs in the clutch means that each egg is weak – there is less yolk – and parents have to care for too many weak offsprings. Clearly, survival chances are adversely affected. Too few eggs also means that the hereditary line faces a greater risk of oblivion than that which has the optimum number of eggs. Because birds who do not get the number right are penalized, we would expect that the surviving birds we observe today have successfully practised private birth control. Interestingly, in the long run, the outcome of such birth control is more survivors, not fewer (Colinvaux, 1978). There is a powerful implication here for human behaviour.

The large young gambit can be extended in terms of parental investment. Thus, unlike birds, babies actually grow inside mammalian mothers. This sort of reproduction gives greater protection to the foetus and, in addition, babies are fed and defended for an extended period. Essentially, there is greater parental investment to increase survival chances of the fewer young (Lovejoy, 1981).

The large young gambit and genes

The large young gambit is particularly interesting because it is the breeding strategy of humans. Like birds and other mammals we practise birth control. We have to. Human females ovulate roughly every month and human males have a sexual appetite that seems to know no season. In other words, we have abandoned a limited breeding season, common amongst many other species, so that we have the potential to have many children.

Just as in birds and other mammals, the success of the human large young gambit depends on a couple starting out with the right number of the young and for the same reason – if there are too many young, the couple will not be able to supply them with enough food resources and all of them will be under-nourished. The couple's breeding effort is wasted. Likewise, if the couple is abstemious, having fewer children than it might have raised, it will contribute less to the next generation than a couple with more ambition. If its fewer children, and children's children, are equally abstemious, then its line will risk dying out. So again the breeding effort is wasted because the goal of hereditary immortality is jeopardized. Ecologists therefore reason that, as far as the ice age humans were concerned, the process of evolution by natural selection preserved those genes that carry the programme to yield the optimum family size.

The large young gambit and intelligence

It is very likely that the ice age humans aided their genes with rational thinking. They followed an extreme form of the large young gambit. The human infant was completely helpless and then had to be nurtured for 10–20 years before he/she was ready to be a parent. The juvenile apprenticeship was very risky as well, so that there was a strong case for rationality in making the family size decision.

It is highly likely that the ice age humans, always reacting to changes in their environment, could read the changes with intelligence. They could also habitually attempt to predict the changes to help them fine-tune family size. Even if the predictions were not always accurate, they could use intelligence with the benefit of hindsight. For example, suppose a family had five children based on its resource predictions but also suppose that the predictions turned out to be optimistic. Then the family could reason that the youngest child was a burden on the rest. There is no point, according to the Darwinian fitness criterion, in having excessive children if they cannot be well provided for. Operating the large young breeding strategy in these circumstances requires a mechanism for culling the excess. Best to kill the last born, the one with the least investment of resources, and thereby increase the survival chances of the remaining. This is the practice of infanticide and we know that the habit was once widespread. Like the intelligence that perceives its necessity, it is a peculiarly human trait. It may be that infanticide is written in the programme carried by human genes. But it seems more likely to be the outcome of reasoned thought which says that infanticide in lean periods can mean more surviving children in the long run. Infanticide then becomes a conscious policy tool with which to optimize family size and thereby confer hereditary fitness. In the same way, contraceptives can also be thought of as an intelligent policy tool with which to optimize family size and ensure fit survivors. If contraceptives do help to optimize and therefore ensure surviving children, then it is intriguing to think that they encourage population expansion.

Interestingly, the practice of assessing the survival chances of the marginal child is carried out today in parts of Africa and also in certain regions of the Indian sub-continent. This variation of a couple's breeding strategy is taken up in Chapter 6.

The large young gambit and cultural selection
Thus far, we have argued that in making family size decisions, couples were aided by genes and by intelligence. To recap, natural selection is a process whereby those genetic characteristics that lead to the optimum family size are retained, the others discarded. The retention and the discarding occurs over a long period of time by the simple way in which those humans that have genes that lead to sub-optimal family size do not survive. Intelligence aids genes since genes cannot forecast, whereas the large-young gambit requires a long period of investment in offspring. Intelligence helps by simulating the future. If, then, genes have dictated a certain number of children but intelligence reckons on one less, then one child may be discarded. Intelligence fine-tunes the large young gambit.

There are various ways in which intelligent use of discretion can be learnt. One is by observation. For example, a young ice age couple would have observed the success and the failure of family size decisions of older neighbouring couples. Observing one neighbour with a large starving family and another with a small, well-fed family, both operating in otherwise similar circumstances, is highly likely to provoke intelligent thoughts.

Intelligent use of discretion can also be acquired by drawing upon the experience of others, in particular the elders in a family, kinship group or clan. In the ice age human society, it is likely that young couples were sufficiently indoctrinated to usually follow the example of their elders, whatever purpose they believed they were fulfilling. In this way, each group developed its own special way of doing things or behaving – its culture. Note that nothing needs to be consciously intended in practising culture: all that is required is that people share cultural traits because it is expected of them.

Consider, now, the process of cultural selection (good references are Boyd and Richerson, 1985 and Durham, 1991). Imagine distinct groups of people living in some given tract of land. Now suppose one group has a culture that is better suited to the rearing of children than that of all the other groups. Then, over a long period of time, people endowed with these successful cultural traits will replace all those endowed with less successful traits. The successful will include not only the original group having the traits, but any other group that may have adopted them. Such people will survive and, with them, their traits. Unsuccessful cultural traits will die out with the dynasties that adopted them.

There is a sizeable short-run problem with the process of cultural selection. Consider a successful culture in which everyone follows its practice. Now suppose some exogenous force changes the environment within which the successful group operates and it is deemed rational to change the culture in response. However, because people are 'locked-in' the culture, it needs some massive effort, perhaps led by a few brave and intelligent individuals, to implement the change. If the group fails to change, then according to cultural selection this group will fail to survive (Colinvaux, 1975).

The problem of the short run is particularly acute if the environment suddenly changes. This is because since many people slavishly follow a culture, sudden adjustment of culture is not commonly observed. This means that a society with a rigid culture may be at a considerable short run survival disadvantage. We have particularly in mind the culture of large families in Asia and Africa and environmental changes such as increased global competition for jobs and resources. Chapter 6 develops this problem further.

The large young plus investment gambit
To the extent that the ice age humans employed tools, they had greater access to resources and as the tools became more sophisticated, their access to resources increased. The parents also taught their children how to use the tools, a rudimentary form of investment in human capital of their children.

Just as the two gambits of 'small egg' and 'large young' depict a quantity–quality trade-off, the 'large young' and the 'large young plus investment' gambits represent an extension of the trade-off. Investment in children is generally costly and its expenditure is meant to replace many low-investment children with fewer high-investment children. To illustrate this vividly let us take a giant leap forward in time and look ahead to decision making concerning family size in the twenty-first century. Suppose the technology with which to exploit the environment becomes more sophisticated and, to operate it, firms seek appropriately trained people. This implies greater investment in children. Of course, intelligent parents will realize, given their fixed earnings, that they will need to reduce family size in order to afford the increased investment. If they do not adjust in this manner, then their hereditary future becomes bleaker. Generally speaking, we can appeal to the compulsion of the survival of the fittest to predict that the optimal family size under 'the large young plus investment' gambit is smaller than that under 'the large young' gambit.

2.4   Rarity of humans in the past

Armed with the preceding concepts from behavioural ecology, we are now in a position to address two fundamental questions of this monograph: one, why we were rare in the past and two, why population always catches up with resources. Consider the former first.

The Eltonian Pyramid

Meat-eating predators, such as lions, wolves and great white sharks, are rare. The constancy of this rarity puzzled ecologists for a number of years but they have now arrived at a plausible explanation under the topic of the Eltonian Pyramid (Elton, 1927). The pyramid is really a pyramid of numbers in nature, with plants at the base. Directly above are numerous tiny animals supporting a smaller army of large animals who in turn support an even smaller collection of even larger animals and so on. It is the structure of the pyramid that ecologists have explained and their reasoning is as follows.

Starting with plants, they trap the energy from the primary source of all energy on earth – the sun. Some of the captured energy is used for building bodies and some for keeping alive. A great deal of energy is also lost as evidenced by fallen leaves and debris. So the animals that eat the plants get only a small fraction of plant flesh. By the same reasoning, meat-eating animals that feed on plant-eating animals must be fewer: it follows that the human hunter, the top predator of the last ice age, was rare.

Humans as hunter-gatherers

The explanation for the Eltonian Pyramid tells us that the population size of a species is determined by the availability of food. For many carnivore species, food supply is determined by specialization. Excellent examples are the black-footed ferret which linked its fortunes to the prairie dogs or the Serengeti cheetah which links its fate to the Thomson's gazelle. On the other hand, being hunter-gatherers, humans, like bears, had access to greater resources and, to that extent, there were more of them. But like bears, being top predators, they were thin on the ground. Things were set to change, however, as human division of labour became greater and technological progress in weaponry enabled us to hunt a wider variety of prey animals.

2.5   Population size and resources

According to ecologists, the relation between resources and population size is approximate. In particular, in the short run, there may be some slack in resources before population expands to remove the slack (see below for details on the mechanism) and sometimes there may be excessive population resulting in population 'dieback'. The long-run causality, however, is one way: it goes from resources to population. Thus, initially resources change and then population change occurs. Some economists are bound to disagree with the direction of causality. They would think that population change can induce a change in resources. Thus an expanding population at the limits of resources may seek innovations to increase the supply of resources.

Why does population always catch up with resources?
Why doesn't population size permanently remain below the resource limit? The two elements of the reasoning for population always catching up with resources are: (1) couples follow the ancient breeding strategy in which the goal is to have the maximum number of surviving children that couples can afford, and (2) there is competition for resources to enable an increased family size so that if one couple does not claim a free resource, then another will.

To see this more vividly, imagine that some natural upheaval opens up a tract of the Sahara desert such that now the soil in the tract is fertile and water is accessible. Then, given (2), people will migrate to the 'new' land (by assumption, all free resources in the 'old' lands will have been captured). The decision problem for the immigrant couple will be that of optimum family size subject to a resource constraint. If the choice is made according to the preferences depicted in (1) then the couple will aim to have the maximum number of surviving children and competition amongst couples for resources to support children will ensure that all the new resources will be captured.

2.6 Conclusion
This chapter has outlined the reasoning, given by behavioural ecologists, for the observation that in our distant past the Earth was sparsely populated with our highly successful ancestors. This is the way the reasoning goes.

1. We humans have a surprisingly great tendency to breed. We have great sexual appetite and we are able to breed throughout the year.
2. On the other hand, our goal is hereditary immortality which means that a couple has to get the family size right. Too many children can overstretch resources and lead to hereditary oblivion.
3. As a result, humans have developed a 'large young with investment' breeding strategy. According to this gambit very few young, as compared to flies and fishes, are raised. They are also cared for a long period of time and, in addition, are given training which is costly in terms of material resources and effort involved.
4. Couples that get the family size right in relation to access to resources survive and enhance their chances of hereditary immortality.
5. To arrive at the optimum family size, couples must have made use of intelligence.

6. Intelligence can be learnt by observing others and it can be applied by following a culture.
7. Successful families will share cultural traits that are conducive to choosing the optimum family size.
8. Cultural selection places families with inappropriate traits at a disadvantage. Such families face hereditary oblivion.
9. So the four million or so humans that populated the earth 10000 years ago and had ancestors going back two million years or so must have possessed those genetic and cultural traits that confer survival success.
10. To take every opportunity to maximize family size and thereby enhance hereditary immortality our successful ancestors must have captured any free local resources.
11. Competition for resources amongst couples will have ensured the disappearance of any slack in resources.
12. As a result, the overall number of humans was fixed by the access to resources.
13. By the reasoning of the Eltonian Pyramid, resources for us, the top predator, were scarce.
14. Hence there were relatively few, albeit highly successful, ice age humans.

So, by the processes of natural and cultural selection, the surviving ice age human couple must have got its breeding strategy right. The human species occupied the top hunter-gatherer niche in the scheme of ice age natural world. There were comparatively few of us. A consequence of human rarity was the absence of spatial overcrowding. This meant an absence of external effects such as environmental degradation (see Chapter 7 for an exhaustive list and discussion of overcrowding externalities). It also meant that private family size decisions were also socially optimal decisions. As a consequence there were no social population problems, such as the prisoners' dilemma population problem in which the social optimum differs from the private optimum.

For perhaps 100000 years human numbers stayed steady. Over the following 10000 years, the numbers accelerated from four million to nearly six billion. Clearly we next need to analyse this incredible explosion.

3 Moving down the Eltonian Pyramid

3.1 Introduction

For 100000 years human population size was more or less constant but 10000 years ago it took off. At first it grew slowly, then picked up speed and more recently the growth has accelerated. In short, we are witnessing an exponential growth curve in the making.

To ecologists and biologists, such population growth curves are not surprising – they repeatedly come across exponential growth in laboratory experiments and field observations. Furthermore, they have fashioned an explanation for the population growths they have observed. This chapter applies their explanation to human experience. An explanation for animal species is not expected to carry over to humans without modification, of course. Bearing that in mind, there should nevertheless be rich and valuable insights to ponder.

The ecological explanation rests on three key concepts of niche, niche-spaces and territoriality (as well as that of gambits introduced in Chapter 2). These concepts are introduced and systematically applied in the initial part of this chapter. At the same time, elementary economics is brought in with the ideas of specialization and the price mechanism. The result of all this analysis can be summarized in terms of food (or more generally resources) surplus (see section 3.7).

Having dealt with positive analysis, we next look at welfare implications. The relevant ecological result here is that any increase in population leads to more people living in poverty. Therefore, mass poverty is the norm. However, alongside the majority living at subsistence level, there is usually also an affluent minority. Its presence suggests the possibility of raising overall welfare and it is explained in section 3.8 how a reduction in fertility rates may accomplish that.

The last part of this chapter examines the environmental consequences of population expansion. Here the concept of a niche is particularly useful. The entire argument of this chapter is summarized in the final section.

3.2 The concept of a niche

It is a significant feature of the natural world that each species occupies a unique niche. It is best to think of a niche as a place in the grand scheme of things. So, in the Savannah, the niche of a cheetah is everything it does to survive (that is, get its food) and thrive (raise its cubs). To be able to do that it must fit in within the Savannah eco-system and co-exist with the other denizens of these grasslands.

Ecologists would say that the cheetah's Savannah niche has been fashioned by natural selection, meaning that the cheetah does what it does well because it has adapted to the Savannah. The process of adaptation is such that suitable cheetahs manage to survive and pass on their suitable genes, unsuitable cheetahs perish with their unsuitable genes.

Niches in the natural world can be likened to professions in an economy. Cheetahs, giraffes, zebras and so on, have their niches just as athletes, security guards, teachers and so on, have their professions. Taking the analogy a little further, the cheetah's niche can support only a certain number of cheetahs just as in an economy only a certain number of people can have jobs as teachers. In other words, there is an upper limit on the number of niche-spaces in a niche or jobs in a profession.

Territoriality
The number of a given species in nature does not fluctuate a great deal. This is because the number of niche-spaces in a given niche is fairly stable. It is clearly instructive to examine how the number of niche-spaces is regulated in nature (in section 3.6 we shall examine types of niche-spaces).

In nature, animals of a given species are spaced out so that overcrowding is uncommon. It really means that niche-spaces in a given niche are spaced out and therefore few in number. Ecologists have advanced the idea of territoriality to explain the prevalence of sparse niche-spaces in nature. Consider lions who are carnivores, and also social, just like us. Lions live in prides consisting of adult females, who are related to each other, their offspring and adult unrelated male lions. Pride male lions spend a lot of time patrolling and marking the area in which the pride lives. The pride lionesses rear the young in their area and the males attack any intruding male lions. Each pride gets fixed into its collective brain that their territory or niche-space is where they should be. It is their home. Homes, and therefore prides, get spaced out across the Savannah (see paragraph after the next below).

Territoriality must help in carrying out the large young breeding gambit with great efficiency. After all, the territorial pride has space, den-sites and access to prey for its own use without too much interference from other lions. Territoriality also confers advantages of shelter and protection (for example, keeping the young on familiar terrain where they can avoid other predators when females are away), cementing of pride bonds and minimizing disease (by minimizing contact). That these beneficial factors are conducive to breeding is supported by the fact that the non-territorial (or floating) lions breed badly – nomadic lionesses have a very poor reproduction record. Ecologists are convinced that lions cannot successfully pair and raise young unless they have a territory.

Turning to consider the number of territories in a niche, note that territoriality requires spacing and that space in a given niche is limited. It is however the case that the size of a territory is elastic – it may be reduced to increase the number of territories in a niche. However, it appears that its size cannot be successfully reduced beyond a certain point. Were size to be so reduced then either territorial animals continue to live in peace but starve and breed poorly or territorial disputes break out, fatalities may occur and thereby eventually territorial size increases with capture by the stronger animals. It would appear that overcrowding is not tolerated by territorial species in nature (Klopfer, 1969). (In later chapters we shall argue that while humans have managed to pack more and more households into limited spaces, there have also been external effects of overcrowding – poverty, inequality, crime, violence, social tension, personality disorders, spread of infectious diseases, environmental degradation and so on.) So, although territoriality is not an inflexible arbiter of numbers, it sets an upper limit after allowing for a small non-territorial population. This population, waiting for an opportunity to acquire territories, can subsist. However, should non-territorial animals fail to acquire their own turf, then their dynasties die out (Andrewartha and Birch, 1954).

It is important not to misunderstand territoriality in nature. The behavioural pattern of 'home-making' requires allotting space to each breeding pair. The control of population that results is an accident. Thus lions are not provided with a mechanism for regulating population; they have territories and this actually boosts the number of babies that each pride lioness can rear. That this system should also set an upper limit on numbers is an ironic side effect. Territoriality, and therefore population control, is a consequence of behaviour, not a cause.

In the long-run then, population size in nature is regulated by territoriality or 'homemaking'. This behaviour both reduces population size and its fluctuations, relative to what they would otherwise be. Anticipating the policy chapters of this monograph, there is here the suggestion that a check on human population by a housing–jobs nexus shortage may imply a healthier (and happier?) population than that checked by a food shortage.

Niche of the ice age Homo Sapien
To link up the concepts of a niche and niche-spaces with the population history of the ice age Homo Sapien of the previous chapter, we note that between 100000 to 10000 years ago, the human race occupied a hunting-gathering niche at the top of the Eltonian Pyramid alongside niches suited to bears, lions, wolves and so on. Since resources at the summit of the pyramid were scarce, a niche situated there had few niche-spaces or territories. If there had been surplus humans relative to the territories, then the resources would have been thinly spread and many humans would have suffered under-nourishment. As a result, over time, the weak would not have survived. So, over the long run, the population of the ice age Homo Sapien was determined by the scarce niche-spaces or territories. Moving down the pyramid, the various niches occupied by herbivores would

have supported a larger population because the greater resources available there would have meant more niche-spaces.

3.3   Humans start shaping the environment

For nearly 100000 years human numbers hardly fluctuated. We were a tribal species and lived in small groups, most tribes having fewer than a hundred members. We lived at a temporary home base to which the hunters of the tribe returned with their spoils. A temporary and rudimentary sort of village life had grown up, with the men hunting and the women gathering food and looking after the children (a general reference is Dahlberg, 1981). Throughout this period, humans lived within the parameters of their environment, adapting to changes in the parameters.

About 10000 years ago, many large mammals became extinct all over the world. The reasons for this extinction are unknown but it has been suggested that this disappearance drew humans more into the open vistas. At the same time, humans began to think before instinctively reacting to changes in the environment. They began to use their bodies more effectively, especially their hands. Thus we took the crucial step towards shaping the environment.

Herding and agriculture

The first great change to affect our lifestyle was the discovery of agriculture. (The second was the industrial revolution, the third electrical, the fourth atomic and the fifth may well be the information revolution.) It has been speculated that the discovery may have been the result of a change in the environment, perhaps creating a situation in which, for the first time, innovation had some chance of succeeding. Agriculture seems to have developed independently in at least three or four parts of the ancient world, including the Near East (Polanyi, 1980). Surprisingly, for such a major discovery, farming spread very slowly, moving north and west at the rate of one kilometre a year. Since not all environments are suitable for sustained agriculture, the concept completely bypassed cultures in areas such as deserts which lack rivers.

We learnt to herd animals instead of hunting them at around the same time. Cattle and sheep were kept for meat and milk that supplemented the unpredictable harvests that must have been experienced by farmers who were learning as they went along. Herding allowed us easy access to animals when we felt hungry and it was clearly a more efficient way of using our calories than hunting. Agriculture meant that permanent structures could be erected and large tools made to help till the soil. We also learnt to store food. Big pits could be dug where food was kept cool. For the first time, we had a degree of permanence. Instead of regularly moving to follow migrating animals, we could stay on one site all year round (Ucko and Dimbleby, 1969).

We also increased our food resources manifold. In fact, we were able to tap the enormous food supplies made available at the bottom of the Eltonian Pyramid. By controlling which plants should grow we obtained access to the primary production of the whole Earth. The implications were profound. It meant that a species could occupy more than one niche without speciating. We were now different from the rest of the animals living in their appointed place. We could now take the food of other animals at little private cost to ourselves. In fact, with time, we acquired the ability to change niche at will. This was an enormously significant event in the history of living things on Earth and it also had great implications for population growth. As we shall see, with an increase in niches, niche-spaces also increased spurring an acceleration in population growth (Cohen, 1977).

Not all things changed. Despite this momentous leap, we still held some allegiance to our ancient niche of hunting-gathering. We were adapted to that role by physique, temperament, desires and learnt behaviour. Some of these things, such as an athletic body, were gradually shed by many of us but many of the others remained. One of these was our breeding motive and strategy.

3.4 Breeding strategy

Every couple continued to raise the number of children it thought it could afford. Assured of food resources new generations worked out that more babies could be afforded. The new couples also had no room for ancient customs that kept numbers down. The artificial restraints of taboo and infanticide could be dropped as the young couples sensed that they could afford more children than their ancestors. As the newly acquired food supplies were converted into more babies, human population began a remorseless increase.

Before the evolution of agriculture, about 10000 years ago, the world's population was approximately 4 million and it rose very slowly to about 5 million by 5000 BC. Then, as settled societies developed on a major scale after 5000 BC, it began nearly doubling every millennium to reach 50 million by 1000 BC and grew to 100 million within the next 500 years and then to 200 million at the peak of the Han and Roman empires (about 200 AD).

There is a parallel here with the population experiments done with animal species in a laboratory. Three or four protozoans placed in tubes of plentiful nutrient broth number thousands within days; a pair of fruitflies put into a milk bottle with banana mash soon approaches hundreds so will a few wax-moths put into boxes of wax or flour beetles placed in dishes of flour. There is a similar increase with a mouse couple kept supplied with food and water.

The experience of our history and the results of laboratory experiments (see Pearl, 1927) are reminiscent of the Malthusian hypothesis (see the next chapter) which states that once the constraint of food supply is lifted, most people procreate more. However, human breeding is not straightforward as in laboratory vessels. First, niches and niche-spaces have to be acquired or created.

3.5   The 'Neolithic Revolution'

Specialization

Earlier, we stated that the population size of a species in nature is fixed by what the niche of the species can support, that is, the number of niche-spaces in a niche. Humans were able, after the invention of herding and agriculture, to convert greater food resources into more niches by the device of specialization. Since agriculture produced a surplus of storable food beyond that which the farmers needed to support and reproduce themselves, niches opened up for people to take the food surplus away from the farmers. The first civilizations seem to have been theocracies, with the priests persuading the farmers to give up their surplus food by threatening that if they did not perform the ceremonies, their crops would fail. Some others, having gained a knowledge of poisonous and drug plants, became witch-doctors and medicine men, easily able to take away some of the farmers' food surplus. More and more people became professionals in something that did not involve direct dependence on food but involved persuading farmers to part with their food surplus, either by means of commodity exchange or by force.

An institutional innovation

Within each profession or niche so created to match the expanded food supply, niche-spaces were also created: people simply saw the opportunity to do something else besides farming or herding and took up that profession. To facilitate exchange, people had to live within reach of each other and the first settlements appeared. These expanded as food surplus grew, as villages became towns, and towns made way for the city-state. Within the city-state we made use of architecture and technology to pack more people in a limited amount of space. Thus our new niche-spaces were deprived of the spatial dimension.

One institution which greatly facilitated the living together of many anonymous people in a confined space was the price mechanism. In a city-state food production and distribution had to be organized and so an elementary form of market economy appeared. Food supplies stabilized with hoarding, storing, importing, as well as with rationing by the price mechanism. The packed niche-spaces could be supported.

The combined phenomena of the transition to agriculture, the growth of settled societies, the emergence of cities and various professions, and the rise of powerful religious and political elites, are often called the 'Neolithic Revolution'. During this period, although there were frequent famines and deadly diseases, both food supply and population, slowly but remorselessly grew.

3.6   Broad and narrow niche-spaces

Thus far we have worked with a homogenous concept of a niche-space. Now we distinguish between two types. A lion territory possessing food, shelter, den-sites and space for breeding can be called a broad niche-space. Non-territorial lions can be classified as living in a narrow niche-space, especially lacking in facilities to breed. A more vivid illustration of life in a narrow niche-space is that of a mass of insect species living in a milk bottle well-supplied with food.

When tracing the evolution of human society, the concepts of broad and narrow niche-spaces can be usefully applied as follows. In the city-state of the Neolithic era there had to be governors and the governed. The lives of the organizers-generals, priests, bureaucrats, merchants – were wide ranging and required many resources of the living spaces to sustain them. These rulers had broad niche-spaces. But for the masses there was a constricted way of life that needed few resources of the living spaces. The masses had narrow niche-spaces. Unlike animals, such as lions, not possessing broad niche-spaces did not prevent the masses from breeding.

Niche-spaces and economic inequality
For the positive-minded economist interested in explaining economic inequality there is a simple theory here: inequality is explained by the distribution of niche-spaces. Thus explaining inequality for the period under consideration in this chapter is easy: niche-spaces were bi-modal with the professions whose task it was to organize and govern occupying broad niche-spaces and the people who toiled occupying narrow niche-spaces.

Those who managed to acquire a broad niche-space had plenty of leisure time as their servants did most of the menial work. Moreover, they did not have to pay any of the costs of giving up the activities of their ice age niche for which their bodily and mental mechanisms were made. They could go adventuring. Some of these lucky people also cultivated their minds, invented the arts, explored the sciences and devised ways of living in comfort. A few people also concerned themselves with the welfare of the masses. The masses, themselves, could only eat and toil in ways for which they were not well adapted by natural selection.

Niche-spaces and population size
The majority of the people, the poor as well as the affluent, appear to have adhered to their ancient breeding strategy of having the maximum number of children that they could afford. It meant that as long as the poor in their narrow spaces did not get the opportunity suddenly to become rich, they stayed poor. As for a dynasty that started rich, it eventually became poor as its wealth got thinly spread out. However, the faces of affluent dynasties kept changing as differing dynasties

managed to acquire or seize wealth and occupy broad niches for a few generations.

The relation between niche-spaces type and population size is straightforward. People who manage to acquire broad niche-spaces do use more resources than those in narrow ones, whether these resources are space, food, energy, raw materials or more subtle things. There cannot be so many of the broad niche-spaces as there are of the narrow ones. So, given the overall resource constraint on niche-spaces, there is a bigger population within the larger number of spaces of the narrow type.

China provides an excellent example of a society composed of broad and narrow niche-spaces. There, the development of agriculture and the emergence of a settled society during the Han Empire (2000 BC – 220 AD) was also accompanied by a dichotomy between the ruling elite and the bulk of the population of peasants living in small villages. The main task of the elite seemed to be to ensure that enough food was obtained from the peasants to maintain themselves and the army. As a result, Chinese agriculture supported a small elite in its broad niche-spaces and the masses in narrow niche-spaces tethering on the brink of starvation.

There are parallels between niche-space sizes and the caste system. In ancient India, people of high caste led cultured lives requiring broad niche-spaces. People of the lowest caste were at bare subsistence level, living in very narrow niche-spaces. There were also ranked castes in between. However, each couple raised the maximum number of children it could afford. It sometimes meant that surplus people in high castes were relegated to castes below where they took up less room. As for the lowest castes, they disposed of those babies that proved to be surplus. More recently, the records of the first British conquerors of India clearly show that infanticide was common among the Indian peasants. This was one method by which those of the lowest caste kept their family size down to what they could afford.

3.7   Cycles of food surplus
During the historical period under consideration in this chapter, there were cycles in food surplus (Colinvaux, 1980). The sequence was as follows. There was an initial growth in food resources driven by inventions such as herding and agriculture and by institutional ingenuity such as specialization. This was followed by the creation of additional niche-spaces. However, most people did not discard their ancient breeding habit of having the maximum number of children they could afford. As a consequence, the niche-spaces were filled by an expanding human population and the food surplus vanished. The outcome was more people than ever before living at near starvation level, vulnerable to famines and diseases, until the advent of the next resource–augmenting technical advance or institutional device. This sequence is consistent with the ecological

view that as the resource cake gets bigger, people take the opportunity to breed more and bite out more and more niche-slices and thus population inevitably catches up with resources. However, since it takes a while for population to catch up with an initial expansion in resources, during this initial phase even the masses experience a higher standard of living and can indulge in activities that are compatible with a broader niche-space. Most of the splendid creative activities, as well as qualities such as wisdom, knowledge and empathy that define human civilization, sprang up during such phases. Moreover, when there were surplus resources, some of the better off in society – those occupying broad niche-spaces – concerned themselves with raising the welfare of the masses.

A good illustration is the experience of China. In south China there was a revolution in agricultural production after the fourth century AD. The expansion of settlement into the new rice growing areas in the south allowed population to reach about 115 million in the early thirteenth century (compared with 50 million in the fourth century). The entire period was characterized by mini food surplus cycles. Improvements in agricultural techniques or farming of new land brought only temporary increases in per capita food supply which were quickly counterbalanced by population increases. The Chinese developed the most sophisticated agriculture in the world and by about 1200 China was considered the most literate and civilized country in the world. However, it also had the largest human population and the masses lived on very low levels of food intake.

Considering Chinese history beyond the thirteenth century, disasters like the Mongol invasion which resulted in the deaths of about 35 million Chinese or the massive epidemics in 1586–89 and 1639–44, which killed about 20 per cent of the population on each occasion, reduced the population pressure temporarily. But after about 1600 there is no evidence of any significant increases in yields and although the area under cultivation rose, the amount of food available per person was about the same in 1850 as it had been in 1550. The masses appear to have lived permanently on the verge of starvation (Elvin, 1973).

3.8 Welfare

For the normative-minded economist the characterization of human history with the masses living in poverty most of the time is of great interest; there might be scope for improving human welfare. True, as we have seen, technical progress has the potential to penetrate through to the masses and increase their welfare by broadening their niche-spaces. Unfortunately for the masses, it appears that technical progress is usually accompanied by creation of additional narrow niche-spaces instead of the broadening of existing ones and these new ones are soon filled with increases in population as people perceive the opportunity to increase the number of children they can afford. Of course, it is undeniable that some people do take the opportunity to broaden their niche-spaces and to that extent the proportion of the world's poor has fallen. On the other hand, as predicted by ecologists, the absolute number of the poor has risen. Today, mass poverty is still with us, on a larger scale and in both urban and rural areas. In addition to mass poverty, new forms of overcrowding externalities – spread of new viruses, global ecological effects – also seem to have appeared.

A theme of this monograph is that technical progress has the potential to raise welfare but often the potential is wasted as it largely disappears with expanding human numbers. The task of the welfare economist is to harness this potential. The suggestion here is that an increase in welfare requires broadening niche-spaces which, in turn, means controlling family size.

Boulding's mesa concept
Boulding (1977, p. 291–2) views the earth as a mesa with broad niche-spaces in the middle, occupied by the affluent, and narrow niche-spaces all around, inhabited by the poor. There are several alternative scenarios for the future. In the ecological scenario, the rich successfully protect their broad-niches whereas the poor breed and the surplus falls over the cliff-edge. In a variation of the ecological scenario, the poor successfully invade the middle of the mesa and everyone eventually becomes poor, breeds and the surplus falls off. In the economic scenario, the rich absorb the poor in such a way that the whole society becomes affluent. But it requires the original poor to practise stringent birth control.

We have argued that one consequence of our ability to change niche at will is population expansion. We now turn to another consequence of this ability.

3.9   Peaceful coexistence: the exclusion principle
Both the mathematics and laboratory experiments show that continued strong competition between different animal species in a given habitat is impossible. So nature arranges matters such that different species are kept separate and thus inter-species competitive struggles are avoided. What happens is that a species finds its own idiosyncratic niche. So, in a given habitat there can be many niches with as many different species, but no more, all living together. Ecologists call this 'one species: one niche' idea the exclusion principle, because the owner of a niche excludes all others from it.

An example of peaceful co-existence
It follows that whenever we find rather similar animals living together in the wild, we should not think of competition by tooth and claw, but we should instead ask how competition is avoided. When we find many animals sharing a food supply, we should not talk of struggles for survival. We should observe to see by what trick the animals manage to be peaceful in their co-existence (Goodman, 1975). As an example, consider African animals on the plains. Zebra, wildebeest

and Thomson's gazelles are usually seen grazing together. Zebra eat the long dry stems of grasses for which their horse-like incisor teeth are admirably suited. Wildebeest take the side-shoots of grasses gathering with their tongues in the bovine way and tearing off the food against their single set of incisors. Thomson's gazelles graze where others have been before, picking out ground-hugging plants and other titbits that the feeding methods of others have both overlooked and left in view. Although these animals wander over the same patches of country, they clearly avoid competition by specializing in the kinds of food energy they take. Ecologists think that natural selection is responsible for such peaceful co-existence – each species has 'selected' the kind of teeth that enables it to survive on the African plains.

If peaceful co-existence, not struggle, is the rule of the natural world then, by changing niche at will, humans have shaken off one restraint of the natural order. However, we do not readily discard a niche when we acquire another. In this way we amass niches and in so doing we deny food and space to other species. Peaceful co-existence with other species goes out of the window (Passmore, 1974).

Apart from knocking out animal species there are other environmental consequences of our ability to amass niches. Our history is littered with examples of environmental consequences of significance: pollution of rivers, lakes, seas and the atmosphere, desertification, reduction in forest cover, global warming and so on. While the extent of these adverse phenomena is debatable and the causes are not agreed upon by everyone, there is enough evidence to suggest that the hypothesis – that our ability to change niche at will and, therefore, accommodate an enlarged human population by knocking out other forms of life has serious environmental consequences – cannot easily be dismissed (Thomas, 1983).

3.10 Conclusion

This chapter has introduced the concepts of niche and niche-spaces and the central argument has been that population size is determined by the number of niche-spaces. So a count of niche-spaces gives an idea of human numbers. This is the fundamental ecological insight into the subject of population. However, there is a twist. There are different types of niche-spaces with the implication that broader niche-spaces imply a smaller population than that implied by narrower niche-spaces, both being constrained by the same amount of resources. Unfortunately, our history has been characterized by an exogenously driven increase in resources followed, with a lag, by an increase in niche-spaces most of which are narrow. Given the lag, our history has had short episodes of food surplus. During such episodes, humankind has had the inclination to pursue those activities that advance civilization. In addition, a minority has taken the opportunity to broaden their niche-spaces. This observation suggests another valuable ecological insight: if greater welfare goes with a broader niche-space then policy-makers should attempt to convert any surplus resources into broadening niche-spaces. This would also restrain population growth by restricting the number of narrow niche-spaces.

The stepwise reasoning of this chapter has been as follows:

1. For about 100000 years, human numbers were stable. Life expectancy was short and a high fertility rate matched a high mortality rate.
2. But then, 10000 years ago, by chance perhaps, humans learnt to increase resources by learning to herd and farm.
3. Not all humans were farmers because by the ingenious device of specialization, niches were created for soldiers, tailors, governors, merchants and other professions.
4. Another ingenious device – the price mechanism – was simultaneously developed in a rudimentary form enabling, say, merchants to pass on grain to tailors in exchange for clothes for farmers.
5. In other words, with an increase in resources went an increase in niches.
6. Most people adhered to their ancient breeding strategy – having the maximum number of children they could afford – so that population caught up with the increase in niche-spaces.
7. The expansion in population was also accompanied by the development of two classes of niches: narrow (or subsistence) niches for the masses and broad (or affluent) niches for the privileged minority.
8. Although most people did not change their breeding behaviour, some had servants and therefore leisure time. A few of these began to think about philosophy, sciences and the arts and began to break the stranglehold of genes on human behaviour.
9. In addition, during the brief periods of food surplus, the masses also had the opportunity to indulge in such activities and contribute to civilization. Some families also broadened their niche-spaces.
10. This suggests that if surplus resources can be diverted away from creation of new narrow niche-spaces, then civilization can progress and people can live in broader niche-spaces. Population growth would also be checked.
11. By our newly acquired ability to 'change niche at will', we encroached upon niches of other species. Whereas in nature species co-exist in a given habitat by occupying non-competitive niches, we simply overran niches when we transformed habitats. Thus began the end of peaceful co-existence between humans and others.

12. There were also adverse environmental consequences of our ability to amass
     niches. However, it is likely that these had not manifested themselves in
     an acute form by the time the Americas were discovered by the Europeans.

At first sight, what happened next seems to have been contrary to the
expectations of ecologists. Economists, however, were quick to move into the
lacuna created in our explanation of population events.

PART II

ECONOMIC ANALYSIS

4 Malthusian economics versus the demographic transition

4.1 Introduction

The previous chapter looked at our population history from an ecological perspective. At the micro level, it was assumed that households are driven by the goal of hereditary immortality and operate in an environment of uncertainty. At the macro level the outcome is that population size hits the resource constraint and any increase in resources permits greater population size. If resources follow an exponential growth curve then so does population.

The ecological perspective is quite plausible when one examines early human history in which the influence of genes is expected to dominate that of the brain. However, in more recent times, it may be expected that human decision making is increasingly influenced by intelligence. In fact, a cornerstone of modern economic theory is rational decision making and this chapter brings in economics as it turns to look at the European population experience in the eighteenth and the nineteenth centuries.

During this period, economics as a subject of study was being taken seriously, thanks to the efforts of economists such as Adam Smith, Ricardo and Malthus. Towards the end of the eighteenth century, Malthus forged a substantial connection between economic analysis and population. In retrospect, it appears that Malthus the economist had adapted an ecological approach to the topic of population. (More recently the school of neo-Malthusians appear to have forged a neat synthesis between economics, behavioural ecology and population.) However, it appears that although Malthus had got the logic right, the assumptions on which his analysis was based were too pessimistic. This means that his predictions were out of line with the European experience. All this forms the subject matter for sections 4.3–4.5.

This was the opening for economists to grab the central stage in the study of population. Based on the experience of Western Europe, a theory of a sort was assembled (section 4.6, 4.8). Unsurprisingly, the makeshift explanation has been heavily criticized by the neo-Malthusians (section 4.7). The differences between the two schools are important because of the vastly different policy implications. In addition, even if the economists may have obtained an important insight into the subject of population growth they may have completely missed out on the topic of population size.

The entire argument of this chapter is summarized in section 4.9.

4.2   European population history

Whereas in the previous chapter, which looked at our more distant past, we drew upon examples from Asian history to illustrate the concepts and insights from behavioural ecology, in this chapter, which looks at our more recent past, we call upon European history for further stylized evidence (Cipolla, 1963). First, consider the Greek civilization, centuries before the rise of Alexander the Great. These were the years of technical advance and expanding the frontiers of civilization as well as rising population and social strife. It appears that Greece resorted to establishing colonies by conquest to absorb her population overflow; in the absence of major agricultural innovations, Greece had to expand her colonies.

After Alexander, the Greek Empire quickly disintegrated. The Roman Empire, which was built later and in a like manner, lasted longer, probably because many of the Roman conquests were of Barbarian lands. Being underdeveloped, they could absorb Roman population overflows for a longer period of time.

Early modern Europe showed signs of overcrowding. In 1300 the population of Europe was 80 million, having doubled from 36 million in 1000, and many parts were severely over-crowded – Northern Italy, Flanders, Brabant and the Paris area for example. European agriculture was a low productive system that improved rather slowly and the shortage of land (the supply of new land was virtually exhausted in the early thirteenth century) combined with the rising population was causing cereal prices to rise and many people must have lived at a very low level of subsistence. Was European population beyond the optimum that could be supported by the technology and the institutions of the time? At the beginning of the fourteenth century there is clear evidence of falling population brought about through permanent malnutrition and near starvation in many areas of Europe from Tuscany and Provence to Normandy and south-east England. The major famine of 1316–17 added to the number of casualties but the pressure of population on resources was not removed until after the outbreak of the Black Death in 1346 and the subsequent recurrences of the plague for the rest of the century. Interestingly, there is some evidence that the age of marriage and the number of unmarried rose when the population was nearer the limits of food production and fell when population pressure eased following famine or epidemic disease.

The period from the late fourteenth century until the mid-fifteenth was one of comparative prosperity as population remained below the peak of 1300 for about 200 years. However, by 1600 it had bounced back to nearly 90 million, slightly higher than in 1300, even though there had been little improvement in agricultural productivity. The signs of 'overpopulation' and an imbalance between food supply and numbers re-appeared. Thus in England agricultural prices rose from about 1500 as shortages started to develop and real wages fell by a half in the period 1500–1620. By the 1620s population growth slowed down as malnutrition and higher mortality caused by inadequate food supplies took their toll. The same symptoms can be found in France. By 1570 most usable agricultural land was in production and, although numbers were kept in check by the continual civil wars of the period, a crisis was reached early in the seventeenth century. Food prices continued to rise, land holdings got smaller and real wages fell drastically. Population rose on occasions to about 20 million but fell back rapidly since at that level it seemed to be out of equilibrium with the number that could be fed in the long term. A series of severe famines between 1690 and 1710 demonstrated that population was still higher than that which the agricultural system could regularly feed.

The sequence of events in such historical episodes is, by now, familiar. First of all, people discover a way of suddenly increasing resources, either by innovation in technology or by devising institutions or by conquest. That opens up more niche-spaces and more resources are also made available for existing niche-spaces. The increase in leisure time consequent upon more resources leads to advances in civilization – greater enlightenment, more precision in knowledge, creative works of art and so on. But this honeymoon period doesn't last. Most people in both broad and narrow niche-spaces continue to follow the ancient breeding strategy, that is, they choose to have the maximum number of children they can afford. The majority do not choose family size consistent with the expanded way of life. As a result of population growth, resources become scarcer and competition for resources becomes fiercer. Those living in broad niche-spaces perceive threats to their way of life from the inhabitants of narrow niche-spaces. Not surprisingly, in order to preserve their affluence, rulers advocate wars in order to conquer new lands, thereby reducing competition for resources and hence threats to their niches. Sometimes, famines and epidemics come to their rescue.

We now turn to connecting such insights derived from behavioural ecology with economists in sympathy with such insights.

4.3 Malthus
Malthus's most famous work, *Essay on the Principle of Population*, was published in 1798 (Malthus, 1798). The essay contained a theory of population that became highly controversial.

Preferences: the connection between Malthus and behavioural ecology
Accidentally perhaps, Malthus forged a connection between economics and behavioural ecology and, at the micro level, that connection is in the description of human preferences. Thus when Malthus wrote about the human tendency to reproduce he meant that preferences are such that, under a vast range of circumstances, couples would prefer to have more children than fewer. When behavioural ecologists refer to Darwinian breeding habits they allude to these

very same preferences. However, like conventional economists, Malthus emphasized the resource constraint on behaviour.

In the comparative statics part of his analysis, an increase in the resources of the household translates into more children. Thus, if for some reason the husband's wage increases, the couple opts for a larger family. In the above reasoning, Malthus was assuming a virtual absence of a trade-off between children and other parental consumption in the preferences of the masses. Contrary to Malthus, modern economists would contend that people's preferences are such that there is, in fact, such a trade-off (see Chapter 4). Malthus's assumption makes sense if children are viewed as primarily a vehicle for hereditary immortality. A trade-off between children and other parental consumption makes sense if parents largely view children as consumer goods that is, having, watching, interacting with their children makes parents happy and is the sole purpose for having them. Incidentally, a trade-off between children and public services (such as social security provision) makes sense if parents regard children as producer goods (for example, children serve as insurance).

Boulding's Dismal Theorem

Malthus went on to trace the aggregative consequences of household behaviour. He first noted that human populations, like all natural populations, tend to increase in an exponential manner. He next assumed that food production grows much more slowly. As a consequence, he reasoned that population would outstrip food supply. With an 'oversupply' of people competing directly or indirectly (via jobs) for food, wages would fall.

It is at this point that Malthus's analysis can be connected with that of Ricardo. According to Malthus, an increase in population leads to greater competition for jobs which means lower wages. That would lead to an increase in the rent for land. Ricardo disagreed. He contended that the fall in wages resulting from a rise in population would lead to an increase in profits. However, both agreed that the working poor would grow poorer and the rich would become richer as a result of an increase in population (see below for elaboration).

A lower wage should reduce fertility rates. But Malthus thought that a time lag would be involved. During the transitional period, there would be starvation, disease and war and these non-price mechanisms would check population growth and could even reduce population size. The influence of starvation on reducing population is best illustrated by the failure of the Irish potato crop in the late 1840s causing about half a million people (about 6 per cent of the total population) to die of starvation. As for disease, the 'Black Death' of the fourteenth century was responsible for killing at least 25 per cent of the population. Finally, war, and in the Second World War about 25 per cent of Poland's population was annihilated (Douglas, 1991). *If* starvation, disease and war ultimately result as a consequence of overpopulation then clearly these are inhuman mechanisms for regulation. Furthermore, it is likely that some families could also practise infanticide in order to regulate family size. Boulding (1977) has encapsulated this outcome in his neat Dismal Theorem: if the only check on population growth is starvation, then population will grow until it starves. The Dismal Theorem and all that it entails should alert modern welfare economists to the possibility of welfare improvement. Human suffering (and possible waste of resources) due to starvation, illness and wars need not occur and infanticide should not be necessary. A task of the welfare economist is to reduce such hardships and thereby increase human welfare.

Boulding's Utterly Dismal Theorem
It is worth noting that Malthus allowed for some technological improvements to take place. But his microeconomic analysis implied that such technical change would lead to increased reproduction and so, in the long run, its benefits would be soaked up. There would be short run benefits to humans but Malthus anticipated the ecologist's argument that small 'aristocracies' would be able to capture a sizeable share of the benefits and enjoy a higher standard of living over the long run. However, the masses would eventually sink back to their narrow niche-spaces. Once again, Boulding (1977) has neatly captured this result in a corollary to the Dismal Theorem, the Utterly Dismal Theorem: if the only check on population growth is starvation, then any technological improvement will have the ultimate effect of increasing starvation as it allows a larger population to live in precisely the same narrow niche-spaces.

Malthus and economic inequality
Making use of Boulding's mesa metaphor (see Chapter 3, section 3.8), we can explore the topic of Malthusian population analysis and inequality. In the Malthusian model, the minority of the rich occupy the affluent territory centred in the middle of the mesa, with a barbed wire fence around them. In some unspecified way, they are never short of resources with which to prop up their affluent territories. Meanwhile the mass of the poor all around them breed to the point where they push each other off the edge of the mesa.

There is, however, an alternative scenario that should help put Malthus's thinking into perspective. Suppose the poor manage to capture the affluent territories and eventually the whole mesa becomes one huge mass of narrow niche-spaces with lives of poverty and misery. Malthus had, in fact, witnessed the French Revolution and had been greatly disturbed by it. As a consequence, he thought that a society characterized by inequality was preferable. Better still would be a society in which the masses had smaller families. However, he did not think that government could help the poor accomplish the goal of smaller families. He placed the burden of responsibility on the individual household.

If households behave responsibly then, in the visual image of the mesa, the rich would still hold on to their affluent territories in the middle, but the masses would not fall over the edge and, in fact, enjoy a higher standard of living.

4.4 The influence of Malthus on Darwin

In October 1836, a 28-year-old Darwin, having returned from the round the world trip in the *Beagle*, happened upon Malthus's essay on population. (In 1854 Alfred Russell Wallace, a naturalist and collector 14 years younger than Darwin, also read Malthus's essay as Darwin had done 18 years before. Independently, he also hit upon natural selection of variable organisms as the driving force of evolution.)

Some observers say that Darwin was the ideological heir to Malthus. What struck Darwin about Malthus's population analysis was the reasoning that since human beings reproduce themselves many times more rapidly than they can increase their necessary food supply, the binding food constraint implies competition for existence among members of the human race and the consequent slaughter of the weak. Darwin was aware that there is competition for existence among animals and plants. Reading Malthus, the idea came to him that competition would preserve favourable variations in wildlife and destroy unfavourable ones. Combined with the occasional occurrence of chance mutation, Darwin reasoned that natural selection would give rise to new species.

4.5 Malthusian outcome postponed?

Malthus strongly believed that there was a tendency for human numbers to outstrip resources. This belief was based on two basic assumptions. One was our tendency to breed. Given the persuasive evidence, most observers would agree that, up to a point, geometric population growth is the innate result of all healthy living. However, Malthus was wrong in assuming that food production arithmetically increases. There is the evidence of the past two centuries which shows that increases in food production depends on land availability and technical progress and it is difficult to predict the path of technical progress. Malthus also underestimated the agricultural potential of the New World lands.

At the time that Malthus was writing, there existed vast tracks of fertile but uninhabited land in North and South America, as well as Australasia and Africa. As this land was put to use, food and raw materials poured into nineteenth-century Europe, encouraging late Victorian economists like Alfred Marshall to virtually ignore natural resources and to concentrate on labour and capital in economic analysis. As a consequence, the Malthusian outcome appears to have been postponed.

If Malthus was correct in his analysis but wrong in his timing, will the problem of mass poverty and misery occur after human population has colonized every tract of useful land? It all depends on technical progress, which has had an unimpeded run, and environmental resilience. Further technological advances appear to be on the cards. What we are not sure about today is the extent to which we can make technical progress without impoverishing the resilience, adaptability and regenerative power of the environment.

In any case, something significant happened in European history; as Western Europe grew prosperous, fertility rates fell. Such a phenomenon, known as the demographic transition, is highly appealing, a win–win occurrence, and thus deserves closer examination.

4.6   The demographic transition
Three phases are involved here and the change from Phase 1 to Phase 3 is called the demographic transition. The three phases are described below, with illustrations from Western Europe's population experience.

Phase 1 – high mortality and fertility rates
Prior to the seventeenth century, Europe's population was characterized by high (about 4 per cent) mortality and fertility rates for centuries.

Phase 2 – low mortality and high fertility rates
During the seventeenth to the nineteenth centuries Europe saw a reduction in mortality rates, as well as an increase in life expectancy (Fogel, 1994, p. 233). Around the time of the Industrial Revolution, the population growth rate in Europe was about 1.5 per cent per year (such growth translates into a 6–7-fold increase in population over two centuries).

Two points concerning Europe's experience are worth emphasizing. One is that the population expansion was accompanied by industrialization in most Western European countries. It also means that population expansion was accompanied by economic prosperity. Second, some of the population overflow was taken up by the natural resource-rich Americas and Australasia. North America, in particular, turned out to be a large supplier of food grains. With the later colonization of the African continent, the supply of raw materials to Western Europe received a further boost.

Perhaps a digression into the causes of a fall in mortality rates is useful. It used to be thought that the trend to lower mortality was due to advances in: (i) public-health reforms; (ii) medical knowledge and practices; (iii) personal hygiene; (iv) prosperity (see United Nations, 1953); and (v) decline in the virulence of pathogens (see United Nations, 1973). However, it is likely that the most important factor was better nutrition (McKeown, 1976 and 1978). Incidentally, Malthus assumed a fixed life span which is clearly false in the face of falling mortality and rising longevity.

Phase 3 – low mortality and fertility rates
After a delay of a century or two, fertility rates also fell in Europe. The change from Phase 1 to Phase 3 is called the demographic transition and it is said to

be complete when both mortality and fertility rates are low and equal to each other. If the transition is accompanied by increased prosperity then it has an appealing visual sequence in which the protective fence surrounding the rich in Boulding's mesa gets pushed out, absorbing the poor, until it rims the entire mesa and the whole population is, on average, prosperous.

Critics, neo-malthusian in particular, have been quick to point out that there is a problem in interpreting the European experience in the light of the demographic transition phenomenon. They think that the transition remains incomplete because Europe's population has always been growing, albeit slowly. If fertility rates do not fall further then population is likely to continue growing, largely due to increases in life expectancy as a result of changing life-styles (for instance, reduction in smoking, further improvements in nutrition, increases in exercising and concern with fitness). Are the consequences serious? Suppose that the population of Europe increased by merely half a percentage point every year. But even this amount, compounded over a long period, is sufficient to take up a lot of space and increase crowding. Furthermore, if technical progress fails to deliver then prosperity could also decline.

4.7   The demographic transition – a theory?
Many economists consider the demographic transition phenomenon, or at least the fertility decline aspect of it, as more than mere description (Chesnais, 1992). They view it as a macro theory of the way fertility rates always automatically adjust to improved circumstances. Briefly, according to one version of the theory, decreases in mortality occur first, largely due to exogenous factors. Then, economic growth ushers in prosperity and although that initially makes rapid population growth possible, it also brings it to an end. However, critics point out that:

1. The theory is largely based on the European experience and therefore, in part, on European culture. If so, can it be universalized in a straightforward way? While the experience of South East Asia may support the notion of a universal theory or demographic transition (see Chapter 9 for detailed discussion on this), Central Africa with its own peculiar culture could provide telling evidence to the contrary.
2. If prosperity changes fertility behaviour and if it is the poor classes in a country that tend to have larger families then, for demographic transition theory to work, economic growth needs to be accompanied by greater economic equality.
3. The theory is silent on the source of prosperity. We think that it is largely based on continual access to underpriced natural resources and continual technological improvements that have little costs of implementation and negligible adverse external effects. It appears that prosperity came easily for

countries that had the technology and the initial access to abundant natural resources – countries of Western Europe, North America and Australasia for example. It may turn out that for the latecomers, today's third world countries, access is limited. In addition, the latecomers face more binding environmental constraints. A vivid illustration is presented by Daly and Cobb Jr (1990). Suppose that per capita consumption level of the average Indian has to rise to that of the average Swede for Indian fertility rate to fall to the Swedish level. Then, India's biomass capital could disappear and other environmental consequences (for example, flooding due to the removal of forest cover, erosion of hillsides, crop destruction due to unpredictable weather, and so on) could also be substantial. This point about a worsening environment–prosperity trade-off is a particularly important one today.

As for continual technological progress, two points are relevant for the prosperity of third world countries. One is that observers in the West are unsure if technological progress can be managed without risk. It is now a complex affair and it is not clear if, for example, nuclear leaks can be contained or genetic engineering can be controlled. With this uncertainty, it is likely that trickle-down effects to the third world are uncertain as well. Secondly, to take full advantage of the technical changes of the future, a massive investment in a country's human capital stock may be necessary. It is not clear how this investment can be financed.

4. The other major trade-off featured in this monograph is that between prosperity and overcrowding. Suppose prosperity is accomplished in all third world countries and that demographic transition takes place. Then eventually it could turn out to be a very crowded planet with substantial overcrowding externalities. Would greater prosperity compensate for these externalities?

4.8 Europe's fertility decline – micro decision making

Notwithstanding criticisms of the macro theory of demographic transition, there has been a secular transition to low fertility in Western Europe. How does one explain this fertility decline in terms of decision making at the household level? (In Chapters 8–10, we shall enquire if the decline can be replicated elsewhere.) Accompanying the fertility decline, there was technological change, industrialization, urbanization, and so on, which meant that the constraints facing the household must have unexpectedly changed, causing revision in the plans of the household. Although we have at hand a micro-ecological theory of household fertility decision making we do not have a micro-economic one (this will be presented in Chapters 5 and 6), so the following points explaining fertility decline are tentative and suggestive.

1. With reference to micro-ecological decision making, couples changed their breeding strategy from the 'large-young gambit' to the 'large-young with

human capital gambit'. The background to this change is as follows. The large agricultural sector in Western Europe used to employ unskilled labour. However, both the increase in agricultural productivity and industrialization raised the relative demand for skilled labour, resulting in greater demand for education and on-the job training. For parents, there was the obvious increase in the cost of child-rearing resulting in, *ceteris paribus*, fewer children. Couples still went for the maximum number of children they could afford but now they could afford fewer of them.

2. There was an increase in the opportunity cost of the wife's time. The reduction in the relative size of the agricultural sector and the increase in that of the industrial sector, together with urbanization, brought women closer to paid market work. For an increasing number of women, the market wage became an additional component of the opportunity cost of having an extra child. Once again, an increase in economic cost causing a decrease in fertility is consistent with ecological thinking since couples still go for the maximum number of children they can afford.

3. Children lost some of their insurance value. Workers in the industrial economies of Europe expected to earn a secure industrial wage so that they had a reduced need to fall back on their children to make up for any unexpected losses in earnings. In addition, state-sponsored social security started to appear, further reducing the need for children to provide old-age support. This reason for fertility decline, which emphasizes the benefits of having children as opposed to the costs, has found considerable favour amongst economists. It is further developed in Chapter 6.

4. Children became less valuable as producer goods. Living in the new urban environment meant that children had fewer opportunities to contribute to the household's productive activities. So, once again, the benefits of having children fell. This is further elaborated upon in Chapter 6.

5. Children acquired greater value as consumer goods. There may have been a shift in tastes with people placing greater value on children as simply a commodity to enjoy. Then, with diminishing marginal utility assumption, the incentive to have an extra child falls with the number of children. Note that if this is the sole motive for having children then it clearly contradicts the biological motive, that is, children as vehicles for hereditary immortality, since it means that couples do not opt for the maximum number of children they can afford. This view is formalized in the next chapter which also looks at the more recent population experience of the West.

To accommodate the transition, an institutional change took place: families became 'nuclearized'. It is possible that had this institutional change not accompanied the fertility change then household decision making would have become frustrated and the fertility transition aborted.

4.9 Conclusion

From an ecological perspective one can state that population numbers are determined by the number of niche-spaces. Any increase in population size beyond that will be temporary. However, the number of niche-spaces themselves are determined by available resources which are continually being augmented by technical progress and ingenious specialization. Thus a population die-back or crash of a Malthusian kind is continually being postponed. If, in the meantime, the demographic transition is completed in industrialized economies and extended to other countries then the Malthusian crisis need not ever take place. However, it could turn out to be a very overcrowded planet with unpalatable overcrowding externalities. The logic in support of the above argument is as follows.

1. The human history – illustrated by the Greek and Roman civilizations – has been characterized by sudden increases in resources, accompanied by increases in niche-spaces, followed by gradual increases in population as people have held on to their ancient breeding strategies. Whenever population has caught up with resources, the result has been competition, social tension and wars.

2. Malthus can be thought of as a scholar who formalized this cycle in his essay on population. In addition, he argued that in the ensuing competition for resources, only the best-equipped would survive. Starvation and wars would take care of the unfit.

3. Darwin, on reading Malthus, was struck by the idea of competition and survival of the fittest. He thought that, together with the occurrence of chance mutation, such competition in the natural world would give rise to new species.

4. However, as far as human competition for resources was concerned, Malthus did not foresee the availability of greater resources, first made possible by the exploitation of the natural wealth of the new lands and then by the Industrial Revolution.

5. Therefore, although population expanded to fill the additional niche-spaces created by acquisition of greater resources, and areas of the world became crowded, there was no Malthusian population die-back.

6. Malthus also thought that the rich classes practised restraint and had fewer children than the poor classes who did not. However, he would have been surprised at observing the phenomenon of the demographic transition: rising prosperity is eventually accompanied by falling fertility. He believed that the poor squander the opportunity to become prosperous by having more children.

7. Fertility decline may have resulted from rising costs of child care as economic growth took place. This was not forseen by Malthus.

8. However, behavioural ecologists should be satisfied with the above reason for fertility decline since this is still consistent with couples opting for the maximum number of children they can afford.

9. Another reason for fertility decline, which is distinctively economic although not inconsistent with ecological thinking, is that prosperity was also accompanied by environmental (e.g. urbanization) and other changes (e.g. transition to nuclear family) which reduced the benefits of children to parents: Malthus did not foresee this either.

10. Taking stock, one is struck by the realization that, broadly speaking, there is in fact no inconsistency between Malthus's prediction of crisis and the observed experience of Western Europe. As long as technological progress takes place so that increases in material prosperity keep ahead of population increases, an outcome of starvation and misery is postponed.

11. If demographic transition happens, is the eventual outcome necessarily optimal? Economists are silent on the normative properties of the population size at which a given country's population will stabilize. Yet, if it stabilizes at 'too large' a number, then we may well have the problem of overcrowding externalities. Suppose that as a result of 'too large' a population, the natural environment loses its elasticity, resilience, and quality as well as becoming smaller. Of course such losses equate with poverty (sic) in rural economies. These and other environmental effects, as well as the vastly important question of optimal population, form the topics of Chapter 7. For the moment we note merely that governments and other agencies are vaguely aware of these consequences of any demographic transition but appear to have otherwise shut them out of their minds.

5   The demographic transition to smaller families

5.1   Introduction

The previous chapter provided two explanations of seventeenth to nineteenth century population experience in the West. It began with Malthus's theory of population and ended up with the theory of demographic transition. While Malthus's explanation is clearly off the mark, the demographic transition theory has been criticized by neo-Malthusians for being incomplete. There is also an embarrassing absence of explicit micro-economic decision making.

This chapter begins by examining the population trends in the West during the twentieth century. It then attempts to explain the variations in the fertility rates by developing a micro-economic model of a rational, selfish couple. (By selfish we mean private decision making without regard to social consequences. In this model, economic decision making involves optimizing an objective in which economic quantities figure, subject to a resource constraint. Interestingly enough, with one alteration to the model's specification, we can also have a micro-ecological explanation for fertility trends. The economic explanation is encompassed in a series of comparative statics exercises in which the effects of exogenous variables on household decision making are worked out.

5.2   The recent population experience of the West

The population of the US has grown from four million in 1790 to 258 million in 1993 – a 64-fold increase. Between 1928 and 1993, the country's population more than doubled, from 120 million to 258 million. The fertility rate in the US has oscillated wildly. The US birth rate was 55.2 births per 1000 population in 1820, falling to 32.2 in 1900. At the time of the First World War the total fertility rate (children per woman) was 3.25, falling to 2.1 at the time of the Great Depression and rising to 2.5 during the Second World War. At the peak of the post Second World War baby boom (1945–65) in 1957, the rate reached 3.7. Since then, it has generally declined.

Although the annual population growth rate has declined, the US has not reached zero population growth. In 1993 it grew by 1.2 per cent – faster than that of any other industrialized country. This added 3.1 million people: 2 million more births than deaths, 0.9 million legal immigrants, and an estimated 0.2 million illegal immigrants. The main reason for the high birth rate is the large number of women (58 million) born during the baby boom period still moving through their childbearing years. Looking to the future, although the total fertility rate has remained low for over 20 years, the effect of the baby boom potential mothers will still be working through the system. In addition, greater longevity will continue to bring about increases in population.

The salient US demographic features are echoed in Western Europe's demographics. For instance, although the birth rates have fluctuated in the short run, the long term trend in most OECD (Organization for Economic Cooperation and Development) countries is downwards. According to the Family Policy Centre in London, birth rate in 1990 was 1.54 per woman compared to 2.6 in 1960. However, like the US, the baby boom effect is still working through and longevity is on the rise. Therefore Europe should undergo population increases in the future.

5.3   Fertility decisions of a couple: the Chicago model

Economists think they can give a reasonable account of observed changes in past fertility rates in the West. Their reasoning is based on the behaviour of rational, selfish couples who respond to changes in the environment in which they operate. In order to unravel the reasoning we need to specify the make-up of a typical Western couple and its environment.

As a point of departure, we consider a simple economic model of fertility along the lines of Willis, 1973. In this model, there is a husband–wife couple who act as a single, utility-maximizing decision maker. Their utility depends on the adult standard of living and on the number and 'quality' of children they have. Adult commodities and satisfaction from children are not directly purchased in the market. Rather, they are produced according to a 'household production function' with inputs of market goods (for instance food ingredients) and of adult time (for instance, time spent cooking, caring for children, going to the movies, and so on). The key empirical assumptions of the model are that mothers are primarily responsible for child care and that children require relatively more of the wife's time than do activities which contribute to the adult standard of living.

Child and adult services

We take it that only two commodities – child services (c) and adult services (a) – figure in the representative couple's welfare. Child services depend on both the number of children (n) and the amount of human capital – education, skills, health – per child (q), and it is convenient to write c as a product of n and q:

$$c = nq \qquad (5.1)$$

Suppose we nominate a benchmark value of 1 for q. In that special case $c = n$ so that then a couple's welfare depends on the number of children alone. This extreme case will be of interest when we consider extremely poor couples who cannot afford any expenditure to increase q. Ignoring for the moment socially provided investment in human capital, the only way poor couples can raise c

is by increasing n, the number of children. Turning to adult services – meals, holidays and so on – we assume that these have to be 'produced' and so require inputs of time and goods.

Cost

Both child and non-child services are costly. The cost of 1 unit of c is denoted by $P_c > 0$ and the cost of 1 unit of a is denoted by $P_a > 0$. P_c has two components: the price of goods (times the quantity of goods) and the price of time (times the amount of time required looking after children). So there is the money cost of child services – food, clothing, housing, transportation, education, health care, entertainment – plus the time cost of child services. Notationally,

$$P_c = P_{xc} b_c + w t_c \qquad (5.2)$$

P_{xc} – index of prices of the market goods and services the couple uses to produce child services.

b_c – the quantity of market–purchased goods and services required to produce one unit of child services.

w – wife's wage rate

t_c – amount of the wife's time required to produce one unit of c.

The assumption of costly child services need not hold in many developing countries; indeed, child services can be profitable. This is because, whereas in the West children do not normally contribute to production in the household, in developing countries children may carry out many productive activities. In addition, in developing countries P_{xc} is lower and w is also perceived to be lower.

In a likewise fashion,

$$P_a = P_{xa} b_a + w t_a \qquad (5.3)$$

P_{xa} – the index of prices of the market goods and services the couple buys to produce non-child services.

b_a – the quantity of market-purchased goods and services required to produce one unit of non-child services.

t_a – amount of the wife's time required to produce one unit of parental services.

Note that the husband's time inputs into c and a are completely ignored in the above formulation. The idea is to explain fertility decisions in the past when the husband had little to do in the 'production' of c and a (he worked at his career) and the wife primarily stayed at home. However, she did have the option of also working for the market wage w, either part or full-time.

Let us define full income as the total possible income the couple can have over its lifetime:

$$wT + V \qquad (5.4)$$

where T is the total time encompassed by the expected lifetime of the wife and w is her market wage rate. V represents the present value of the lifetime earnings of the husband (Y) plus any unearned income accruing to the couple over the period.

The budget constraint, which equates total expenditure with total resources, then is

$$wT + V = P_c c + P_a a \qquad (5.5)$$

and is represented geometrically in the Figure 5.1.

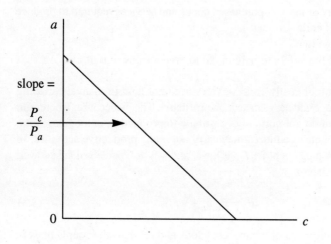

Figure 5.1 The family's budget line

The slope of the budget line represents the market rate of exchange of child services for adult services, P_c/P_a; that is the amount of adult services that needs to be given up in order to produce and consume an additional unit of child services.

Preferences
It is reasonable to assume that the couple's material and time resources are fixed. If so, then the couple can enjoy an increase in child services only by accepting

a decrease in adult services. The implication is that the two types of services are substitutes. If true, it means that a policy-maker can bribe a couple to do with fewer child services by offering them more adult services.

This is a convenient place at which to draw attention to the contrasting assumptions made by economists and ecologists. As we have just noted, economists assume a a,c trade-off in preferences. Ecologists (to take an extreme position) deny such a trade-off. To explain this, suppose there is a poor couple which cannot afford investment in human capital for its children so that $c = n$. Then, in the a,n space, whereas the economist would be happy with preferences depicted in Figure 5.2, the behavioural ecologist would be uneasy about the shape of the indifference curve. He would question the implied trade-off between a and n. He thinks that the overriding motive of most couples is to have the maximum number of children they can afford: beyond a survival level of $a = \bar{a}$, children take precedence over a. The concern of the couple is reproductive success which implies utility success.

Figure 5.3 depicting preferences has been drawn under the assumption that the couple prefers any increase in children no matter what happens to a. Then no increase in a can make up for a decline in n, however small. However, the couple does prefer more a provided no n need be given up to obtain it. Thus if we start with 100 units of a, the couple will prefer any point involving more n than that implied by point A regardless of the associated quantity of a (provided a does not lie below the survival value of $\bar{a}$ e.g. points B, C and D. It will also prefer any point on AE above A (more a with no less n). However, it will consider *in*ferior to A any point to the right of A or on the line segment $A2$ below A. Thus, every point in the diagram other than A is either preferable to A or less desirable than A. There can be no second point that is indifferent to A, so that no

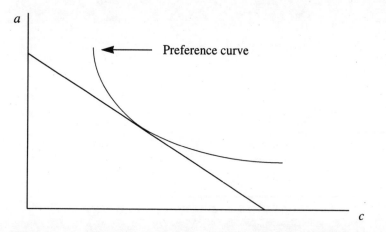

Figure 5.2   The family's budget line, preferences and equilibrium

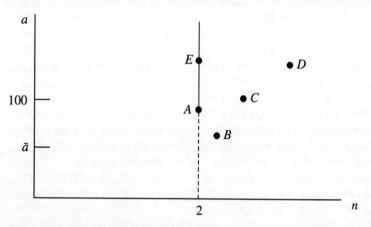

Figure 5.3   Lexicographic preferences

indifference curve through *A* (or through any other point in the diagram) is possible. Clearly, if preferences are as depicted, a policy-maker would find the bribe of adult services to compensate the couple for one less child infinitely costly.

Given such lexicographic preferences, we now add the budget constraint to determine a couple's choice. In Figure 5.4, the couple's feasible set is $0\,\bar{a}XYZ$ and the trick is to find the point that is most preferred in the set. Since $0\,\bar{a}YZ$ can be ruled out of contention we have to restrict attention to $\bar{a}XY$. Here point

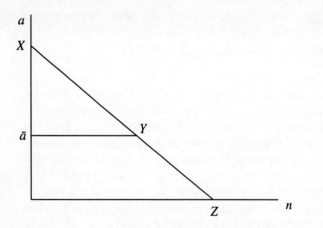

Figure 5.4   Equilibrium for a family with lexicographic preferences

Y has the highest number of children and since no other point in $\bar{a}XY$ has children more than or equal to Y, this point is most preferred.

Returning to the mainstream economic model, it should be pointed out that in this model fertility decision can be embedded in a broader economic theory of the family. In fact, the model has been extended (see, for example, Becker 1981; Cigno 1994) to include analysis of savings and labour supply.

5.4   Comparative statics: a change in V

To explain the broad trend to smaller families in the West, we are restricted to the variables contained in our economic model above. Now variables such as P_{XC}. V and W are not under the direct control of couples. These variables have also changed considerably over the last couple of centuries and may conceivably have influenced fertility decisions. Therefore, we now take changes in these variables one by one and trace out the consequent changes in the couple's economic decision making. Before we do that, note that over the period in question preferences could have changed as well. While this would constitute an explanation of a sort, it is not amenable to economic analysis because the tools aren't there. Interestingly enough, changing preferences is an explanation that ecologists are not comfortable with either. According to them, the desire to have reproductive success is programmed in the genes and such programmes take at least thousands of years to change.

Recall that V is the discounted value of lifetime earnings of the husband plus any unearned income accruing to the couple. When viewed over a very long time horizon, V has undoubtedly increased a great deal in the West. Diagrammatically, the effect of this is an outward shift in the budget line.

As drawn in Figure 5.5, an increase in V expands the resources available to the couple, assuming that the relative prices, P_c and P_a are unchanged. (That is a rather questionable assumption and the next analytical step will be to trace out an increase in P_c). From Figure 5.5, it is evident that an increase in V means that the depicted couple plans to raise its consumption of both c and a.

Quantity–quality (n,q) *trade-off*

There is an important detail associated with the qualitative result just obtained. North American evidence (Mincer, 1963 pp. 75–9, Dooley, 1982, Moffitt, 1984, Fleisher and Rhodes, 1979) suggests that demand for investment in children's human capital rises with parental income whereas the demand elasticity for children themselves, although positive, is close to zero. So with an increase in V a typical couple has virtually the same number of children who are more educated, healthier and so on. Incidentally, note that since an increase in V raises q and that P_c is assumed constant, obviously $P_c q$ rises with V. But since $P_c q = P_c c/N$, the average price of children rises with V.

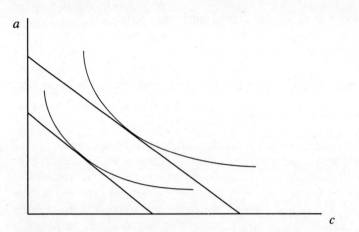

Figure 5.5   The effect of an increase in V *on demand for* a *and* c

(a,c) *trade-off*

The qualitative result that an increase in *V* translates into an increase in *q*, as well as an increase in *a*, depends on the shape of the indifference curves. Suppose now that a couple's preferences are lexicographic, that is, that depicted by ecologists. The relevant diagram for analysis is that given in Figure 5.6 and it shows that an increase in *V* simply translates into more *c* (the old equilibrium point is *B* and new one is *B'*). This result entails great parental sacrifice in terms

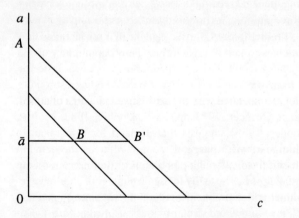

Figure 5.6   The effect of an increase in V *for a family with lexicographic preferences*

of a and would appear unlikely to prevail generally in the affluent West. Here, the affluent citizens do spend more on themselves when incomes rise so that preferences are not likely to be lexicographic. The result with lexicographic preferences does have support elsewhere: we do have instances of parents of Chinese and Indian origins making enormous sacrifices for their children's education, both in Asia and in the West. Such sacrifices may also hold good for other couples in the third world. Nevertheless, the fact that with more resources people do spend more on themselves in the West, suggests that the instinct to breed need not be paramount all over the world.

Explaining the transition to smaller families
The Western couple has a small family whereas the third world couple has many children. This may be a reflection on the difference between child rearing costs. In the third world, where child rearing costs are lower, an increase in V may be accompanied by an increase in n, the number of children. In the West, an increase in V goes with more q – perhaps couples have to invest more in children to enhance their survival chances in the competitive West – and hence the family size stays small. If this is all plausible, then the tendency for large families in the third world and small families in the West is consistent with ecological thinking: the goal is the same (to have the maximum number of surviving children), but the breeding strategies differ to reflect the cost difference of bringing up children.

An alternative explanation concerns preferences. With a sufficiently large increase in V perhaps preferences change from lexicographic to those depicted by conventional indifference curves. Such a change means that people can free themselves from their ancient breeding instincts: they simply enjoy having children and, furthermore, children with more human capital impart greater enjoyment. They can have more children who are capable of reproducing in turn but choose not to. Instead, they spend any surplus resources on themselves. Examples of the taste change could be some people developing a taste for extreme comfort, others for leisure activities and some people finding a substitute for passing on genes – for example, passing on knowledge and works of art for posterity.

5.5 The effect of a change in wife's wage
We now analyse the revised fertility decision of a couple after an increase in the wife's market wage takes place. See Figure 5.7.

There are three analytically identifiable effects: (1) the income effect – the couple is richer- and that pushes the budget line out; (2) a substitution effect – P_c increases making child services more costly (see Equation 5.2) – making the budget line steeper (P_c/P_a increases); (3) P_a also increases (see Equation 5.3)

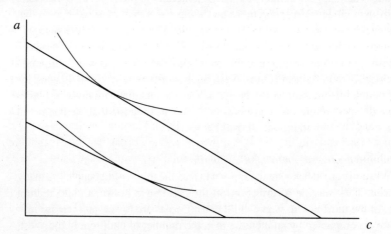

Figure 5.7   The effect of an increase in w *on demand for* a *and* c

exerting an opposite substitution effect which flattens the budget line (P_c/P_a decreases).

The diagram has been drawn to reflect that the combined effect of (2) and (3) is to make the budget line steeper. The intuition for this is that child services should be more time intensive than adult services. Then, when *w* increases, child services become relatively more expensive.

The female cost-of-time hypothesis

The question then is which is greater: the income effect that raises the demand for *c* or the overall substitution effect that lowers the demand for *c*? Figure 5.7 has been drawn under the assumption that the substitution effect is greater so that the overall effect of a change in *w* is to decrease the demand for child services. However, the demand for adult services increases. It means that when *w* increases, adult services are substituted for child services.

The female cost-of-time hypothesis is that increases in *w*, the value of female time, tend to increase the cost of children relative to adult services, causing households to substitute away from children. In addition to expecting increases in the value of female time to reduce *c*, we would also expect women to conserve their increasingly valuable time with additional purchased goods, these being financed by their greater earnings. Given this reasoning, we may speculate that the recent economic history of the West has seen technical progress fuelling economic growth raising market wages and hence the value of time. Such increases in costs of children are bound to have reduced demand for child services.

The quality–quantity interaction hypothesis

Child services have two components, quantity and quality of children so the next logical question is: will adult services substitute for quantity or for quality? Since an increase in w makes the wife's market time more valuable and looking after children more expensive, it is plausible to think that the wife will wish to substitute away from looking after children and possibly the most efficient way of accomplishing this is to have fewer children. In fact, available American econometric evidence supports a negative *ceteris paribus* elasticity between wife's wage and the number of children (Dooley, 1982; Fleisher and Rhodes, 1979; Mincer 1963 and Moffitt, 1984). It is then plausible to think that the expenditure on children's human capital will increase, financed by the wage rises.

Willis (1973) and Becker and Lewis (1973) have also shown that the demand for child quality and quantity interact because the marginal cost of a child is higher the greater expenditure is per child and, conversely, the marginal cost of child quality is higher the more children there are. Thus, if income has a stronger effect on the demand for quality than for quantity, then the relative marginal cost of the number of children will tend to increase as family income increases, causing a substitution effect against fertility which may be more than strong enough to offset a positive income effect in favour of children. Incidentally, this may help explain why higher income families tend to have fewer children.

5.6   The effect of a change in the costs of goods and services

We now analyse the effect of an increase in the cost of purchased goods and services necessary to produce child services on a couple's decision making. Incidentally, it is reckoned that it will cost $86000–$168000 to raise a child born in 1992 in the US to age 18 – a considerable increase in the real cost of raising children over the last century.

Consider an increase in tuition fees, which are a component of P_{xc}. The resulting increase in P_{xc} also increases P_c and so the slope $-P_c/P_a$ becomes steeper. This change is represented in Figure 5.8 from which it can be seen that there is a straightforward decrease in both child services and in adult services. Since $c = nq$, the decrease in c can be met by a decrease in n or q or a combination of the two. It might be difficult to decrease q. There is the possibility that when competing for a limited number of jobs, new entrants may require a minimum amount of q – greater than that required to complete minimum schooling – to stand a realistic chance of obtaining a job. Consequently, the decrease in c is likely to come from having fewer children.

5.7   Conclusion

In Chapter 4 we examined the population experience of the West in the light of the macro-economic theory of the demographic transition. However, the micro-

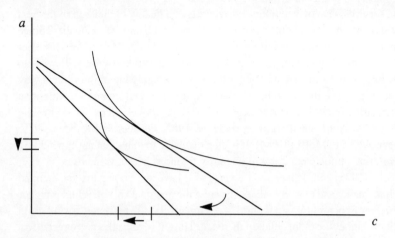

Figure 5.8   The effect of an increase in P_{xc} *on demand for* a *and* c

economic decision making underpinning this theory was absent. This chapter has attempted to rectify this.

The micro model of the household has featured a rational, selfish, decision-making couple. A critical assumption has been that present in the preferences of the couple there is a trade-off between goods and children – you can bribe a couple to have one less child by offering material compensation. Behavioural ecologists would be uncomfortable with this assumption and would deny the trade-off.

The rest of the chapter then traces out the effect of changes in the couple's economic environment on the couple's decision making. In particular, it examines the couple's response to changes in household income, wife's market wage and the price of children's goods and services.

The analysis explains the recent population experience of the West as follows. Rising prosperity has resulted in greater consumption of child services but that has come about mainly in the guise of quality of children. In addition, prosperity has been accompanied by rising child-rearing costs, implying fewer children. So the overall effect is that of having a smaller family. At the same time, expenditure on adult services has increased.

Like the above economic explanation for the trend to smaller families, the ecological explanation can appeal to rising child-rearing costs. However, it is awkward for it to explain greater expenditure on adult services since the goal of hereditary immortality is better served by having more child services at the expense of adult services; it therefore appears that many couples can have more children but choose not to. On the other hand, if it could be demonstrated that it is a minority of affluent couples who behave in this way, the masses continuing to have children and continuing to experience poverty, then the ecological explanation still has credibility. It seems reasonable to entertain the hypothesis that in Western societies there is heterogeneity amongst the adult population.

Despite the trend to smaller families, we shall argue in Chapter seven that the West is already over-populated. Furthermore, note that the West's population is still rising, albeit very slowly. This population growth is partly driven by an increase in longevity. In any case, it makes the problem of overpopulation worse.

Unlike the West, per capita incomes in the third world are low but population growth rates are high. The third world appears to be heading towards overpopulation. What are the reasons for high fertility rates in the third world? Is decision making in the third world different from that in the West? If so, is it because of different preferences or differing constraints? It is these questions that we address next.

Appendix
The micro-economic model of this chapter can usefully be placed into an inter-generational framework. Consider a model in which the life cycle is divided into three stages childhood, adulthood and old age. Assume that parents have children at the beginning of the second stage and during the rest of the period they invest in the health and training of the children. Parents themselves work in the second period and retire in the third.

In order to explore inter-generational transfers, we need a benchmark model. So we assume that (i) parents are altruistic (as opposed to selfish) towards their children in the sense that they care about their children's welfare (in the manner of Becker, 1974 and Barro, 1974), (ii) a perfect capital market in which parents can borrow and lend at a given interest rate, (iii) non-pecuniary returns to education, risk and other complications are disregarded. Then (see Becker and Tomes, 1976 for a formal demonstration and also Daly, 1982 for a sceptical view): (1) the parents maximize the joint wealth of the entire family line by investing in the human capital of each child up to the point at which the marginal rate of return is equal to the rate of interest, (2) redistribute the resulting wealth among family members so as to maximize utility according to the preferences of the parents, and so (according to Willis, 1987) the sequence of privately optimal decisions made by parents in each generation yields the Pareto optimal level of fertility and investments in children from the standpoint of all current and future generations within the family 'dynasty'. The optimal solution is characterized such that:

Net parental expenditures on a given child = (direct and opportunity costs of all the resources devoted to a child's consumption and investment in human capital) + (the value of a monetary transfer made in the next period when the parents are old and the child has reached adulthood).

Inter-generational transfers

If parents are sufficiently altruistic and/or sufficiently wealthy relative to their children then the direction of inter-generational transfers will be from parents to children, that is parents invest in their children's human capital during childhood and make bequests. From an institutional point of view, transfers of this sort are relatively easily carried out within a nuclear family structure in which grown children leave their families of origin and establish independent households.

6   The third world couple

6.1   Introduction

This chapter addresses the puzzling fact that whereas fertility rates have fallen
– or are in the process of falling – in many parts of the world, elsewhere they
have held up. This matters, of course, if there is overpopulation – or likelihood
of overpopulation – and the adverse external effects associated with
overpopulation are serious (see Chapter 7 for an elaboration). It also matters for
economic theory since it casts doubt on the universality of the demographic
transition, a largely economic explanation for transition to lower fertility. To recap
quickly, the demographic transition asserts that there is a third phase in which
fertility declines in response to greater prosperity, following a second phase during
which the lowered mortality of the first phase continues, economic growth
takes off but population continues to increase. The new angle of this chapter is
the possibility that countries can get stuck in the second phase, experiencing
lowered mortality but unchanged fertility while economic growth take-off is
aborted. The failure of sustained economic growth can be attributed to the new
idea that economic development itself depends negatively on fertility rates.

The possibility of a vicious circle of high fertility and poverty
The countries in question are mainly in the third world – sub-Saharan African
countries, a few Latin American countries and some countries of Asia, particularly
South Asia. These countries have not experienced prosperity and it could be
argued that once economic development gets under way, fertility decline will
follow. However, suppose economic development itself depends on fertility (the
demographic transition theory ignores the possibility that high fertility is also
a cause of poverty, inhibiting economic growth). But then how is it that high
fertility did not inhibit economic growth in the past? The answer probably lies
in technical progress. In the case of Western Europe, technical progress enabled
successful exploitation of energy sources of coal and oil, mining of minerals and
colonization of empty, fertile lands. It also made industrialization possible.
Because of the nature of technical progress, it did not matter a great deal that
babies do not arrive equipped with productive human capital – the required
investment in education was not high and the required training period was
relatively short. Parents managed to equip their children with basic human
capital thereby enabling them to contribute to material prosperity and so
overcoming the handicap of high fertility.

Now suppose that we have reached the stage in world development where economic growth for a country depends on production processes that require very high levels of human capital. Then a large, poor family is at a considerable disadvantage in investing in children's health and education. In addition, of course, a large family also consumes more. As a result, in order to engineer prosperity, it would be unwise merely to wait for technical progress to 'happen'. In fact, we might have first to engineer a fertility decline directly and that means, to begin with, an inquiry into the reasons for persistent high fertility rates.

In this chapter, two explanations for large families are offered. Section 6.3 presents the view that people can get locked into social norms that have to do with family size and sections 6.4–6.6 present the household theory of survival uncertainty and large family bias. In the concluding section we assess the above two explanations alongside that arising from the demographic transition theory. But first, a brief look at trends.

6.2   Population trends and projections in the less developed economies

In 1995 planet Earth supported 5.5 billion people, a doubling of world population since 1945. UN forecasts suggest that by 2020 world population will exceed 8 billion, up by 45 per cent from 1995. It is also estimated that in 1995 there were more poor people in the world than ever before – about 1 billion and of these, 0.7 billion suffered chronic hunger. No reliable estimates are available for environmental externalities and overcrowding externalities.

The rapid growth of the world's population appears not to have been caused by a rise in crude birth rates. Rather, it seems largely due to a decline in crude death rates, especially in the less developed countries.

The principal interrelated reasons for this decline in death rates are: better nutrition because of greater food production and better food distribution; fewer infant deaths and longer average life expectancy because of improved personal hygiene, sanitation, and water supplies which have curtailed the spread of many infectious diseases; improvements in medical and public health technology including antibiotics, immunization against infectious diseases, and simple oral rehydration therapy (about one third of all deaths under five years of age are caused by diarrhoea diseases).

6.3   High fertility rates and social norms

According to a World Bank study (1991) the total fertility rate in sub-Saharan Africa has remained at about 6.5 per couple for 25 years and population growth has accelerated from 2.7 per cent per annum in 1965–80 to about 3.1 per cent more recently. Fertility rates in countries such as Kenya are falling but only very slowly. There is the impression that fertility rates are 'sticky'. Two explanations have been advanced for the stickiness and we shall examine them in both this section and the next.

The explanation advanced in this section is associated with Dasgupta, 1993 and is as follows. High fertility rates may have obtained in the past as a rational response to high mortality rates then prevailing. The practice has survived, despite falling mortality rates, possibly because procreation is a social activity, that is, a given household's decision about family size is influenced by the cultural environment (see, for example, Easterlin, Pollak and Wachter, 1980; Cotts Watkins, 1990). This means that for as long as all others in the society follow the practice of large families, no household on its own will wish to break with the practice. However, if all other households were to restrict their fertility rates, each would follow suit. Thus there can be multiple social equilibria, each sustained by its own bootstraps, and a society can get stuck in one which, while it may have had a collective rationale in the past, does not have one in the present.

How could a culture of high fertility have arisen? To answer this, we could resort to the idea of cultural selection introduced in Chapter 1. Suppose that, in the past, population density was low and mortality rates were high. A household following the ancient breeding strategy of having the maximum number of surviving children would respond by having a high fertility rate (instead of a low fertility rate and concentrating parental investment on fewer children). If such a household thereby increased its dynastic survival chances then, in the long run, such households will dominate since households with smaller families will become less populous. This is both because some small households will fail to survive and also some will copy the perceived successful breeding strategy of the large family household. We might then say a culture club of large family households will become established. It is interesting to note in this context that even today in much of sub-Saharan Africa, where rural women lose something like a third of their offspring by the end of their reproductive years, much of their lives is spent in pregnancy or lactation. In Bangladesh about 60 per cent of a woman's reproductive life is spent thus, the corresponding figure in Pakistan being 50 per cent (see McGuire and Popkin, 1989).

In human societies, once a culture club has become established, it has a tendency to grow for non-biological reasons, for instance, if there are economies of scale. An obvious one is group security: the more members there are in a group, the easier it is to defend. Another one is networking: the larger the network, the greater is the benefit per head if specialization can be practised. But not only has a culture club tendencies to grow, it also becomes entrenched. The reason is that mentioned earlier: usually no household on its own has a strong enough incentive to deviate from the culture. A contemporary example is the practice in rural northern India to have a large family. Suppose one newly-married woman desires to break with tradition and have a small family. However, if every other married woman adheres to the custom of a large family, the woman in question may find it worthwhile not to defy the social pressures and punishments. Thus the culture of large family persists.

The argument above assumed that the original reason which gave rise to the culture is no longer valid. However, there is the possibility that there is another reason, perhaps a newer one, which gives rise to the cultural trait of large families.

6.4   Fertility response to uncertainty

In this section, we argue that survival uncertainty imparts a large family bias and that the persistence of this uncertainty translates into large family dynasties. We thus have an alternative reason underpinning a cultural trait and also one that exerts an influence today.

One effect of industrialization in the West was that it increased the chances of biological and economic survival of an average western person. Accordingly, and taking small liberties, the analysis of the previous chapter was carried out under the assumption of certainty. By way of contrast, we now assume that a typical third world couple is economically insecure and faces a future in which its dynastic survival is highly uncertain.

Assume that a typical third world couple wishes to increase the probability of its own survival as well as dynastic survival. Survival requires both good health and economic power. We take it that the couple has negligible assets in the form of finance, land, physical capital and its own human capital. However, the couple may be able to increase the family's stock of human capital by exercising its fertility options. This is a highly credible action if children are viewed as durable economic goods and if the prevalent family structure imparts ties, bonds and obligations between parents and children.

Given uncertainty and meagre resources, how might a couple exercise its fertility options so as to increase the survival chances? To motivate discussion, consider fertility decisions made by couples in the Indian State of Rajasthan. For largely economic reasons, couples regard boys as a more productive investment than girls. Accordingly, a couple will withhold investment in a child until a boy is conceived. So if the first child is a girl, the couple will try again, hoping for a boy and postponing investment in children. As a result, whereas the western couple will stop at two children, say, whether or not they are both boys, a Rajasthan's couple will stop at two boys thereby imparting a large family bias. Continuing with this line of reasoning, and remembering that the Rajasthan couple is looking for the best investment opportunity, it makes sense for it to have its boys spaced out. Spacing out enables the couple to observe the first boy over a period of time to assess his potential and if the child is not promising, the couple can try again. As a result, the couple need not stop at two boys if they are assessed to be unpromising, thereby imparting further large family bias. It is interesting to note that May and Heer (1968) have estimated that an average Indian couple in the 1960s needed to have 6.3 children in order to be 95 per cent sure of having a surviving son when the father reached the age of 65. The study is a vivid illustration of the thinking behind procreation activity in parts of the Indian sub-continent.

For the outlined breeding strategy to work, we need to assume that the boys will honour the 'obligations' expected of them. Such an assumption may be a good one if it is traditional to honour such obligations and the tradition is robust. Robustness is very likely to obtain if the tradition has some optimal characteristics, for example, it pays the children of each generation to look after their parents and, in turn, be looked after (see Samuelson, 1958 and Desai and Shah, 1983). Interestingly, in the Indian sub-continent the proportion of the elderly who live with their children (for the most part, sons) is of the order of 80 per cent or more. The corresponding proportion in the US is about 15 per cent.

It is worth noting that the character of such a breeding strategy is Darwinian in that 'lucky' dynasties have greater survival chances. This is best seen by contrasting two dynasties. In the 'lucky' dynasty a promising son fulfils his potential when adult and uses acquired resources to support his parents and siblings. This chance happening permanently raises the dynasty's survival chances. In the 'unlucky' dynasty, the large family is left to cope with survival with stretched resources.

Finally, note that in the interest of efficiency, that is, getting the best return on investment in children, equality is sacrificed when following the breeding strategy in question. Thus fewer resources are allocated to girls than to boys and, also, boys with promise secure more resources than boys without. This practice of treating children unequally is clearly at variance with western practices.

Political uncertainty
A new angle on survival uncertainty and family size is put forward by Bledsoe (1994). Based on research in rural areas of Sierra Leone, Liberia and the Gambia, she thinks that political uncertainty is an important component of uncertainty facing the rural population. In these countries, there is the constant struggle to cope with uncertainties concerning crop failure, illness, shortages, overnight currency changes, exploitation, fear of losing patronage network, and so on. The majority of the population does not have the conventional stocks of wealth – bank deposits, stocks and shares, land, dwelling – to hedge against disaster. Moreover, centrally provided social security and insurance is negligible. 'Under such conditions, people try to achieve security through the domain of life that offers both diversity and stability: children', Bledsoe (1994, p. 131). She thinks that the diverse skills and social ties which a family cultivates through children enables it to deal with economic problems and political perils. So children and the relationships that they forge with the outside world are a substitute for wealth. If so, having successful children is politically motivated.

Turning to the costs of a family, in recent times costs of education, food and medical care in rural Africa have shot up. Educating a child for any length of time puts a great strain on family resources. Education itself is a gamble, given the high level of unemployment. A rural couple is less sure than before that any one child will be able to remit money. On the other hand, children are of uncertain potential – a few may die, most will barely survive, but one may achieve great success. Families are then best seen as entrepreneurs who adopt a portfolio strategy of fertility. Since parents are not sure about children's capabilities, they will try to retain all options. That means having as many children as possible and then assessing their worth after birth. As children's potential unfolds, investment allocation can be made: children that are most promising will secure the heaviest investment. Hence, by diversifying in children's training, a portfolio strategy is adopted.

Bledsoe is also pessimistic about the use of contraceptives to control the number of births. She finds that many African women adopt contraceptives not as devices to reduce children but for spacing births. So, having decided on the number of children based on portfolio considerations, contraceptives are employed to get the timing right. Since the objective is dynastic survival, if the parental strategy works then it must mean that contraceptives help in raising population size.

6.5   Limited parental investment and child-rearing costs

We have argued that the non-egalitarian breeding strategy as a response to uncertain dynastic survival imparts a large family bias. The resulting large family, of course, requires resources unless infanticide, neglect and abandonment are common phenomena. However, resources required for child investment are relative to costs of investment so that it is proper first to check out costs of child rearing. There are two broad but distinct components of cost: material resource costs and time costs. In the third world rural areas, environmental resources are usually common property so that parents do not bear the entire material costs of child rearing. Furthermore, most children acquire very little education so that human capital costs are negligible. As for time costs, it is usually the housewife who looks after children (with help from older children and female relatives) and it is usually assumed, perhaps incorrectly, that the opportunity cost of the wife's time is low. (Child-bearing costs – pregnancy and the additional risk of death – are also, of course, borne by the wife).

At this juncture it is worth drawing attention to a possible conflict of interest in couples. The fact that men bear little of the time costs of child rearing implies that husbands compensate wives by bearing material costs, thus avoiding conflict between husband and wife. Thus in Northern rural India women are entirely economically dependent on men and bear all the time costs of child rearing. A conflict may arise when working out the number of children to have. If the couple disagrees then the husband usually gets to indulge in his preferences even though his calculations for hereditary immortality may be off the mark. Such free riding at the wife's expense cannot persist since the dynasty is more likely to be headed for oblivion. In the short run, however, it can lower the personal welfare of the wife.

6.6 Limited parental investment and children as producer goods

We have argued that, on average, the costs of children are lower in the third world so that scarce parental resources should not unduly constrain the parents' non-egalitarian breeding strategy. It turns out that, in fact, net costs, that is, costs minus benefits of children, are even lower.

The salient characteristic of relevance here is that, unlike western countries, third world countries for the most part are biomass-based subsistence economies – the rural population being directly dependent on products from nature. Let us consider energy. In rural areas as many as five hours may be spent on gathering firewood, dung (and fodder for domestic animals). In contrast, the direct time spent by households in acquiring fuel (and water) in urban areas is virtually nil. Clearly, labour productivity is low. Children are continually needed as workers by their parents, even when the parents are in their prime. From about the age of six years, children in poor households mind their siblings and domestic animals, collect energy sources and fetch water. In fact, the Centre for Science and Environment (CSE) 1990 study of work allocation among rural households in the foothills of the Himalayas recorded that children in the age range 10–15 years work one-and-a-half times the number of hours adult males work. Cain (1977) studied data from a village in Bangladesh and found that male children became net producers at as early an age as 12 years. He also estimated that male children compensated for their own cumulative consumption by the age of 15. If this is generally true then it means that a child is usually like a free good, sometimes a profitable good.

The value of children as producer goods, of course, depends on the assumption that children have work to do, an activity which is severely limited in times of droughts and famines. It also depends on the assumption that children stay with their parents. After all, if children are mobile, then it becomes difficult for parents to extract resources from them.

At this juncture it is appropriate to mention that children can also serve as an insurance good for support in the event of a disability and in old age. There is some hard evidence for this: using Mexican data, Nugent and Gillaspy (1983) have shown that old-age pension and social security do as a substitute for the marginal child.

Under conditions of certainty, it would appear that children can be profitable: that is, the marginal child's lifetime benefits exceed lifetime costs. Nevertheless, the question of when to stop having children arises in practice. One reason is uncertainty and incomplete insurance markets. There is the probability that a child will not survive to teenage and the expected future benefits will be lost. Therefore, expected lifetime benefits are less than expected lifetime costs. Since no insurance company will insure against such an eventuality in the rural third world, it makes sense to transfer consumption resources earmarked for the marginal child to investing in an existing, promising child. Another reason is imperfect credit markets. Financing initial consumption of the marginal child at high borrowing rates means lifetime benefits are less than lifetime costs.

A consideration of the costs of children has raised an identification problem: is the observed large family size the result of the non-egalitarian breeding strategy, or is it due to low net costs of children *per se*? All we can do is confirm the existence of the identification problem and assert that the non-egalitarian breeding strategy is not constrained by the net costs of children.

6.7   The Caldwell Hypothesis

The impression that net costs of children are lower and benefits higher in the third world than in the West is highly credible (Dasgupta, 1993) and instances of profitable children abound in the rural third world. In these cases, the transfer of resources over a life cycle in poor, rural families is from children to parents. This is, of course, in sharp contrast with advanced industrial nations where the transfer goes the other way. In this context it is interesting to note the observation of Caldwell (Caldwell, 1976, 1977a, b, 1981, 1982) that whether a country has made the demographic transition is related to the direction of the transfer.

The Caldwell Hypothesis requires the assumption that selfish parents are interested in maximizing profits equal to the value of net transfer of resources from children to them. So, if the value of the transfer due to the marginal child is positive, then the couple will have that child. This strategy requires parents to have sufficient power vis-à-vis their children to be confident that they will be successful in extracting transfers from children. The power is likely to be derived from social customs.

Now suppose something that is beyond the control of the parents occurs – for example, urbanization or development of labour markets – which reverses the flow of transfers because of extraction problems. Then parents will have fewer children. Not only that, parents will also reduce investment in children (see Willis, 1994).

The point about investment reduction renders the Caldwell Hypothesis implausible, for it is generally observed that families with fewer children invest more than families with more children. Some observers also think that children are generally not profitable under conditions of uncertainty so that a key assumption of the hypothesis is unrealistic. Ecologists think that, in any case, parents are not primarily interested in making profits from children. They are simply interested in maximizing dynastic survival in the face of uncertainty. When they cannot extract as many resources from children as before, they cannot afford a large family so the family size shrinks. However their breeding goal and strategy otherwise stays intact so that investment in best prospects is held up.

6.8 Conclusion

This chapter has focused on the (micro) decision making of a third world couple. Unlike the western couple, the procreation decision is made under the assumption of uncertain dynastic survival. In economic parlance, the objective is to maximize probability of dynastic survival subject to limited parental resources. This, in fact, is a refined form of our ancient breeding strategy (see Chapter 2).

We have called this breeding strategy a non-egalitarian breeding strategy and argued that it imparts a large family bias. It is non-egalitarian because children are not treated equally as far as allocation of resources are concerned: boys, being better earnings prospects, are invested in more heavily than girls and, in a similar vein, promising boys command greater investment than unpromising boys. This strategy imparts a large family bias because to ensure the selection of promising boys you need a large pool of children from which to select. This strategy is feasible because in the third world costs of rearing a large family are low, enabling even poor couples to indulge in it.

Explaining high population growth rates in the third world

Mortality rates have fallen in the third world whereas fertility rates have not. The result has been high population growth rates in the third world. We have three possible explanations for high fertility rates:

1. Couples in the third world are locked in a culture club which arose in a high mortality environment. The club sanctifies large families and it is difficult or costly for a couple to leave the club unilaterally. Couples want to have smaller families but cannot exercise their choice.
2. As a response to survival uncertainty, couples in the third world are following a non-egalitarian breeding strategy that imparts a large family bias since the expected private benefits of a large family exceeds the expected private costs.
3. Third world countries are at Phase 2 of their demographic transitions so that the observed high fertility rates are temporary.

The third explanation is favoured by most economists. The underlying reason is that prosperity induces a fall in fertility. Since prosperity is usually accompanied by industrialization and urbanization, rising child-rearing costs, greater investments in human capital, a reduction in survival uncertainty, taste change, and so on, it is difficult to be precise about which mechanisms are at work and with what effect. Two serious questions arise: suppose that somehow prosperity can be engineered, how long will the transition take? Furthermore, will it lead to an overcrowded third world with the attendant adverse externalities? The second question is: is prosperity inevitable? Demographic transition for the third world comes up against a stringent environment constraint which implies that prosperity is virtually impossible for every country. This is partly because if industrialization means a depletion of the bio-mass then the rural population must become poorer. To be sure, some section of the society will become richer as a result of such an industrialization process but mass poverty is likely to remain. In which case, the demographic transition mechanisms have little chance of working. Societies then can get locked in Phase 2 (see Brown *et al*, 1987). One way out might be to reduce consumption and that means an independent reduction in fertility.

The second explanation works on the expected private benefit of a large family outweighing expected private cost. As long as that remains – and underpinning it is the presence of survival uncertainty – large families will prevail and hence population growth rates will hold up. If it is survival uncertainty that gives rise to large families and this practice is followed in a routine manner, that is, it becomes a cultural trait, then the first explanation, while it may have been relevant in the recent past, has been superseded by the second explanation. In other words, couples do not wish to overthrow the culture of a large family.

PART III

NORMATIVE ANALYSIS

7   Overpopulation

7.1   Introduction

World population is predicted to increase in the short, medium and the long run. Population growth rates, of course, vary across countries. In fact, a few western European countries and Japan face a gentle population decline. Many more countries are expecting falling birth rates although these are still expected to exceed the replacement rates so that their populations should continue to grow. The important examples are India, China and Indonesia. The main thrust to population expansion will come from these countries and countries in Africa and Latin America where fertility rates appear to be sticky.

Third world population projections do look daunting. Of course, predictions often turn out to be false. On the other hand, an air of inevitability hangs around population trends into the future. Optimistically, one could say that the currently observed population J-curve will eventually turn into a sigmoid curve, implying that world population will finally stop growing and stabilize. However, given that today's children will be tomorrow's adults and will wish to have children in turn, it could take a long time with the consequence that it turns out to be a crowded planet.

This chapter ignores the problem of population growth leaving that task for Chapter 9. Instead, it addresses normative questions of the following sort: what is overcrowding (section 7.5)?; and what are the mechanisms whereby overcrowding reduces welfare (sections 7.6–7.8)? In other words, it tries to identify the problem of overpopulation, that is, the situation in which population size is greater than optimum size. It also attempts to persuade that the overpopulation problem is serious and that individual households lack incentives to do anything about it in the course of their normal behaviour. Therefore, collective action has to be considered and so the stage is set for the policy chapters that follow.

7.2   The sigmoid curve: population growth in a confined space

Experimental biologists, interested in the effects of overcrowding, have conducted laboratory experiments on this subject. The idea has been to introduce a handful of fast-breeding couples, of fruitflies say, into a container of food. The question posed by such an experiment is this: what happens when the supply of food is increased given that space is fixed?

The scientists have found population growth to follow a sigmoidal (after the Greek letter sigma) or s-shaped curve (Krebs, 1988). Initially, when there are only one or two pairs of fruitflies, they reproduce very quickly, making babies as fast as their bodies will allow. Soon there are one or two dozen breeding pairs and they raise healthy families in turn. As the multiplied numbers are themselves multiplied, the population starts to leap ahead (all the while the container being kept well supplied with banana mash). But finally the rate of increase begins to slacken. Eventually, the numbers in the pressing crowd of flies remain constant.

It appears that the sigmoid shaped population history has something to do with crowding. In the early days food plus plentiful space creates excellent conditions for breeding. In the next few generations, conditions are still good and so the fruitflies breed flat out. But eventually all this breeding raises a crowd. Now parents have to compete with others for food and so spend their energies in strife. Consequently there are fewer calories for reproduction, reducing the birth rate. Females get less to eat in crowded bottles where the surface of the banana mash is crowding with flies and hungry females lay fewer eggs. There is also evidence that the maggots and pupae tend to die in a banana mash wriggling with other maggots. Some stressed adults might also die, increasing the death rate.

Some similar experiments carried out with flour beetles showed that they suffered additional inconveniences. Crowded flour beetles were discovered to eat their own eggs by mistake as they blundered through the flour. The blundering beetles also bit into each other and into their own maggots. A pair seeking to copulate in a corner of the crowded flour would often not get the job done before being bumped by another beetle.

Results are not only similar, in particular that the population growth is sigmoidal, with mice kept in a small enclosure and continually supplied with food, but more spectacular. For example, in a hopelessly crowded mouse enclosure, the complicated social life needed to sustain a mouse mother collapses so that she cannot look after her babies any more. Furthermore, crowded male mice can develop unsatisfactory symptoms, ranging from orneriness to a state of sullen shock.

It is not difficult to predict that there would be greater hardship if food supply was reduced. Thankfully, we have not come across an experiment in which food supply was progressively reduced but it is almost certain that a population crash would follow, an instance of Malthusian crisis.

Here is a summary of this section. First, organisms have an inherent propensity to breed and if unchecked, exponential population growth results. However, the environment – space and resources – eventually sets a limit to growth. As a result, populations of organisms in the laboratory grow as a sigmoidal to reach a stable number that needs to be continually supplied with food resources. One can only imagine what life must be like in this overcrowded environment – most likely miserable.

7.3 The J-curve

Armed with the background of the previous section, we now turn to human population growth. Throughout most of history, human populations have been relatively small and slow-growing. Studies of hunting and gathering societies indicate that the total world population was only 4 million people around 10 000 years ago. That was just before people learned to domesticate animals and invented agriculture. Prior to that, human numbers had been fairly stable for about 100 000 years. However, after the agricultural revolution, population slowly grew, reaching about 5 million people by 5000 BC and archaeological evidence and historical descriptions suggest that about 300 million people were living at the time of Christ. Thereafter, fertility rates picked up but checks in the form of plagues, famines and wars meant that in 1650, at the end of the last great bubonic plague, there were only about 600 million people in the world. However, as Figure 7.1 shows, population began a rapid increase after that. During the Renaissance, human population entered an exponentially increasing pattern of growth – a J curve – and continued up the curve during the Age of Reason. Notice from Table 7.1 that population doubling times diminished correspondingly.

Clearly, the world population is exhibiting a J-curve type exponential growth. In 1987, population passed five billion with an estimated doubling time of only 35 years. Looking ahead, there are four possibilities that are interesting to consider:

1. We are on the upward slope of a population overshoot.
2. We can continue the present trend indefinitely.
3. Overcrowding will enforce self-regulation and our population growth curve will exhibit a sigmoidal curve
4. Our agents, governments for instance, will intervene to successfully regulate population growth and size.

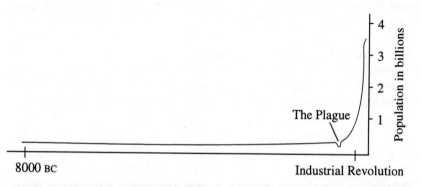

Figure 7.1   World population growth as a J-curve

Table 7.1: *World population growth and doubling times*

Date	Population (millions)	Doubling time (years)
5000 BC	50	?
800 BC	100	4200
200 BC	200	600
1200 AD	400	1400
1700 AD	800	500
1900 AD	1600	200
1965 AD	3200	65
1990 AD	5300	38
2020 AD (estimate)	8230	55

Source: Population Reference Bureau, Inc., Washington, DC.

Consider the first possibility. In the natural world, as opposed to laboratory experiments in which food supply is easily topped up, there are limits to exponential population growth. When a population exceeds the carrying capacity of its environment or some other limiting factor comes into effect then death rates begin to exceed birth rates. Population biologists call this the dieback (see Hendrick, 1984) or population crash. The extent to which a population exceeds the carrying capacity of its environment is called an overshoot, and the severity of the dieback is generally related to the extent of the overshoot. This pattern of population explosion followed by a population crash is called irruptive (see Berryman 1981). We could call it Malthusian growth. The reason, as we have seen (Chapter 4), is that Malthus thought that human populations tend to grow until they exhaust their resources and become subject to famine, disease or war. Neo-Malthusians – most biologists and many social scientists – today think that natural population regulation by resource-driven checks and balances also applies to human populations.

7.4 Food supply and population growth
A great deal of suffering must be involved when population growth follows a J-curve and is then regulated by resource constraints. However, there is the second possibility of following the J-curve indefinitely. Recall that in the laboratory experiments food was continually supplied to laboratory organisms and population grew to match the food supply. Looking at our recent history, over the nineteenth and the twentieth centuries food production grew more than six times whereas world population has increased sixfold (the food surplus has been absorbed by an increase in per capita food demand in the affluent West). More recently, there have been fluctuations in food supply but the trend has been

upward (see Mitchell and Ingco, 1993). It is also interesting to note that today wheat is cheaper, in terms of other commodities, than it was in Malthus's time. Indeed, the relative price of staple foods vis à vis manufactured goods is expected to fall in the near future to reflect a reduction in the costs of food production. Hence, to the extent of this cost reduction incentive, suppliers are likely to raise output of food. All the economic indicators therefore appear to convey that as we move into the twenty-first century, food production will increase. If the human population problem is seen as that of the Malthusian fear of world population outrunning world food supply, then at a first glance there does not appear to be a cause for immediate concern.

However, there are three worries. One is the prediction of increase in food supply which applies to the world's food production. It is difficult to see how most major developing world regions can increase their food production appreciably. Sub-Saharan Africa faces great difficulties in raising food production by 2–3 per cent every year as does the Middle East. China, too, is likely to face a slowdown in its food production growth. It may turn out in the future that such world regions will import food from food surplus Europe and North America. While countries of the Middle East, Asia and South America may be able to finance their cereal imports, this is less likely in the case of sub-Saharan Africa.

Earlier we stated that food supply can be influenced by costs of production. According to some economists, food supply is also driven by effective demand (that is, demand backed by purchasing power) which Africa lacks. So if Africa is unable to buy extra food then the large scale undernourishment in Africa will worsen. Note that behavioural ecologists believe that effective demand is of minor importance. They think that food production is driven by technical innovations and any surplus gets mopped up by the demands of a growing human population. So the current increase in third world population is simply a catching-up effect. If so, then in a highly uncertain future there is the possibility of an interruption in the growth of food supply and hence a population dieback.

If food supply is driven by efficiency then there may, in fact, be a way out for Africa in the short run and that is to raise management performance and thereby raise Africa's food production. In other words, there exist unexploited opportunities to raise production. If corrective policies – making relative prices more favourable to food production, improving irrigation, expanding agricultural research, providing more complete insurance and credit markets – were put in place, then sub-Saharan Africa should be able to raise food production (see Sen, 1994). However, for misery on a vast scale to be eliminated, food supply growth will persistently need to exceed population growth.

The second worry concerning food supply has to do with the external effects of an increase in food production. First, it is thought that extending the margins of arable land will impose stress on the natural environment. In poor rural areas, farming is usually extended to less productive and more environmentally fragile areas (for example, forests and hilltops). Second, farming more intensively may mean an unsustainable use of chemical fertilisers. Such problems are not confined to the third world; some analysts (Crosson and Anderson, 1991, for example) believe that today the problem of sustaining food production at acceptable environmental cost is a global one unless new, environment-friendly, techniques appear. However, grave doubts are emerging concerning human capability to manage the use of *any* new technology safely. Two general (that is, non-food) examples are management of nuclear energy and that of genetic engineering. While the first world has a good record of preventing nuclear leaks, the second world has not. As for genetic engineering, these are uncharted waters in the sea of technology and no one knows if the escape of genetic material – accidental or deliberate – can be prevented.

The third concern with food supply is more philosophical and it arises from doubts about our ability to take corrective action. There is no guarantee, even if food supply matches human needs for food, that food will not be wasted and that societies will not horde and risk destroying food in order to benefit from speculation about food prices. The general point is this: while it is widely accepted that human beings have great potential, it is also generally acknowledged that human energy can be massively misdirected. It seems that the social institutions that underpin human society can be highly imperfect – history is littered with such examples.

To sum up, nearly two hundred years ago, Malthus was wrong to have feared an imminent population crash due to mass starvation. He had reckoned without fully appreciating human ingenuity to discover new agricultural lands and increase crop yields on existing cultivated areas. Whether the increase in food supply is driven by technology or by effective demand inducing innovation is not important in demonstrating that Malthus was way off mark. But was Malthus wrong over the long term (more than two centuries)? Is the party finally over? We have given three strong reasons to think that this is an important question which should not be dismissed lightly.

7.5 Maximum versus optimum

When the world's population was two billion fifty years ago most people would have expressed great concern at the prospect of a doubling or trebling of the world's population. However, technological progress and human ingenuity conspired to accommodate the larger population. Suppose now that our population growth curve resembles the S-curve with population size stabilizing in the future at, say, 50 billion, a shade over nine times the estimated 5.8 billion population of 1996. (At the arbitrary figure of 50 billion one imagines that even human ingenuity has reached an environmentally imposed limit. It is widely accepted that for human capabilities to work, you need a resilient environment and ecologists think that presently we are not too far off the limits of environmental resilience.) With a world population of 50 billion it is likely that a sizeable majority would be existing on a diet of grain, indicating a lowered standard of living. There would also be, most likely, adverse external effects of overcrowding, further reducing human happiness. These references to the standard of living suggest that asking how many people can the Earth support is asking the wrong question. It is somewhat like asking how many cigarettes can one smoke before contracting lung cancer. In any case, packing more people in a given space is a technological achievement, not an economic one. A more appropriate question appears to be: what is the optimum world population?

The answer depends on the objective function or the welfare criterion. We have worked with two: that of dynastic survival (Chapters 1, 2 and 5) and that of happiness (Chapter 4). The objective of dynastic survival or having the maximum number of surviving offspring may appear consistent with a world population of even 50 billion. However, it is most likely not consistent since, with such a large population size, the survival chances of all are greatly diminished. The optimum population relative even to this criterion is likely to be smaller.

The other objective function we have worked with is that of utility derived from consumptions of parental services and child services. Does population size adversely affect such utility? The answer is yes if there are external effects arising from population size that adversely affect utility via an additional argument in the utility function. For example, this argument could stand for 'overcrowding' which people generally dislike. Under such circumstances, the optimum population is determined by considerations such as this: whereas an increase in children increases child services and therefore happiness, if the collective effect of such independent, household decisions transmitted via externalities reduces happiness by more, then the population size exceeds optimum size.

Of course, we have not answered the question of the optimum population size with any precision. Our stance is that reducing adverse externalities moves us to the optimum. This can be accomplished by either reducing the external effects directly or decreasing population size. For our analytical purposes this is enough. A qualification, however, is in order. In thinking about reducing adverse externalities due to population size we shall ignore a transitional problem concerning age structure. The problem is that in making the change to a lower population, there results a disproportionate number of the old, placing a heavy burden of economic support on the young

Clearly our next task is to take a closer look at external effects of population size and we begin with an externality that probably matters more in the West than in the third world.

7.6   Overcrowding externality and inefficient consumption

Let us begin with overcrowding externalities that directly reduce people's utilities and, for the moment, assume that any environmental limit on population size is not binding. Overcrowding may imply a loss in quality of life. Three important ingredients of quality are space, liberty and an absence of stress, tension and anxiety. Space links to quality via preferences – most people 'mind' traffic jams, crowded shopping centres, crowded beaches and other such recreational areas and so on. Crowds can be a public 'bad' if individuals value freedom and liberty. This is because, for a given society, an increase in population means an increase in regulations. With more people, interactions between people increase and that can lead to more social problems so that additional rules, regulations and laws have to be introduced. But with extra regulations, freedom of action is curtailed. People 'mind' such loss of liberty and hence 'mind' overcrowding. As for stress, recall that in laboratory experiments it was observed that each beetle or fruitfly or mouse had to fight to get food, mate and so on, when the laboratory vessel became congested. Stress in mice was observed and, as a result, the mice developed unsatisfactory symptoms. We may speculate that in overcrowded human societies additional stress can also be present, and to that extent, society's welfare will be lowered.

Analytically, it proves useful to say that people 'mind' the cumulative loss in quality of life which results from overcrowding and we can then insert an overcrowding term inside a measure of welfare such as a utility function. However, there is a limitation: in some societies people like having people constantly around them. This could well be a cultural feature and we have to restrict our analysis to not to apply to such cultures.

Consider the ith household and let household size be given by n_i. Summing over all households in the economy, $\Sigma_i n_i$, gives us the economy's population size $N = \Sigma_i n_i$. Let c stand for a measure of overcrowding or congestion in the economy. Congestion depends on population size N and we may write the congestion function as

$$c = c(N), \qquad c'(N) \geq 0 \qquad (7.1)$$

$c'(N)$ is the effect on congestion resulting from an increase in population. The possibility that at low population size congestion may be absent is captured by the use of the weak inequality in equation (7.1).

We now come to the reason for congestion mattering and that means a description of individual preferences. An individual is assumed to value space – the more there is of it, the happier is the individual. This assumption can be specified more formally by placing the congestion function into the individual i's utility function:

$$u^i(a_i, n_i, c(N_{-i})) \qquad u_n > 0, u_c \le 0 \qquad (7.2)$$

where a_i is a consumption bundle: we have simplified here by ignoring household production. Furthermore, it is assumed that child services are proportional to n with the factor of proportionality set at unity. Since we want to focus on external effects of population size, nothing of essence is lost by the simplifications.

The presence of $c(N_{-i})$ in the utility function above means that an increase in the country's population, which increases congestion, can cause further unhappiness. But the property of $u_c \le 0$ allows for the possibility of a sparsely populated country and we have ruled out $u_c > 0$ by assuming that the country at hand is not a desert island. Note the presence of N_{-i} instead of N in the congestion function when it is inserted into the ith individual's utility function. It means that the individual household does not cause congestion on itself but adds to the congestion inflicted on others. The individual's budget constraint is given by:

$$a + pn = v \qquad (7.3)$$

where v is exogeneously given income, price of a is normalized at unity and p is the relative price of n.

We now directly address the question of optimum population and proceed by defining a social welfare function over the utilities of the Z households in the economy:

$$U = U(u^1(.), \ldots, u^i(.), \ldots, u^n(.)) \qquad (7.4)$$

where $u^i(.)$ is given by equation (7.2). This is maximized by the social planner subject to

$$\sum_i a_i + p\sum_i n_i = \sum v_i \qquad (7.5)$$

and the first order conditions are:

$$n_i : U'u^i_{n_i} = \lambda p - \sum_{j \ne i} U'u^j_c c'$$

$$a_i = U'u^i_{a_i} = \lambda, \lambda \text{ being a lagrange multiplier}$$

or

$$\frac{U^i_{n_i}}{U^i_{a_i}} = p - \frac{\displaystyle\sum_{j \neq i} U^j_c c'}{U^i_{a_i}} \tag{7.6}$$

The presence of

$$\sum_{j \neq i} U^j_c c'$$

in equation (7.6) informs that when deciding on family size, the social planner takes into account the congestion impact each individual household has on others.

We now compare equation (7.6) with the corresponding behavioural rule under individual household optimization. Formally, the individual maximizes equation (7.2) subject to equation (7.3) by choosing n and a, taking $c(N_{-i})$ as given. The first order conditions are:

$$n : u_n = \tau p$$

$$a : u_a = \tau, \ \tau \text{ being a lagrange multiplier}$$

or

$$\frac{u_n}{u_a} = p \tag{7.7}$$

The absence of

$$\sum_{j \neq i} U^j_c c'$$

in equation (7.7) indicates that the individual household fails to take account of the lowered satisfaction of other households resulting from its impact on overcrowding. The reason is that, by assumption, the others' utilities do not matter to it.

The above formulation yields some measure of welfare loss – it depends on the shape of the congestion function, the structure of individual preferences and the specification of the social welfare function. It means that the above society could move towards optimum population if:

1. People change preferences and stopped 'minding' overcrowding so that the extant population becomes the optimum one. Incidentally, societies do exist where people relish crowds.
2. Some technological change reduced overcrowding effects (better public transport, urban planning, and so on).
3. There were fewer people.

It is worth dwelling on the last. The above formulation assumed that: (a) happiness matters, (b) people have a choice concerning family size, (c) private decision making leads to overcrowding and (d) overcrowding more than reduces the happiness an extra child could yield. As a result, people would be better off with a smaller family size. However, the incentive to do so is lacking: a family is not sure that if it reduces its family size then all the others will follow suit; and if the others don't why be a sucker since you lose out on happiness associated with an extra child but have to contend with overcrowding anyway. So individuals acting unilaterally cannot do anything to capture the extra happiness which is there. There is scope for collective action though.

Finally, note that in the above formulation we have been concerned with the short run consequences of a shortage of space, burden of regulations on social behaviour and stress. There are also bound to be long run consequences of a build up of, say, stress. One cumulative consequence is violent conflict.

7.7 Overcrowding externality and inefficient production
With overcrowding there is greater competition for resources and, in laboratory experiments, it was observed that each fruitfly or beetle or mouse had to expend great energy to get to the food. As a result, the animal species were undernourished. Taking this cue, consider the following rural third world situation. Economists have insisted that in many rural societies children are also regarded as producer goods. The Indian Centre for Science and Environment, (CSE, 1990), reports that villagers in central Himalayas spend 30 per cent of working time on crop cultivation, 20 per cent on fodder collection, 25 per cent on fuel collection, animal care and grazing, 20 per cent on household chores, and 5 per cent on miscellaneous activities such as marketing. Children contribute in large part to these productive activities. Now, in the cases of fodder, fuel collection and grazing, it is usually the case that there is free access to the environment. But, in the circumstances in which the local environment is degraded and the number of working children is large, exploiting the environment is far from easy. With too many children competing for too few resources, there may be a loss in production efficiency in that fewer children would be able to

collect more resources than many children. In that case, the standard of living would be higher for the village as a whole. Lets set out the dilemma more formally.

Consider a third world rural society. Any of the households, assumed identical, can procreate at little cost. Let n_i denote the family size of the ith household, $i = 1,2,...,Z$. Then the village population is given by:

$$N = \sum_{i=1}^{z} n_i \qquad (7.8)$$

which can be usefully re-written as

$$N = \sum_{\substack{j=1 \\ j \neq i}}^{z} \hat{n}_j + n_i, \quad \hat{n}_j \text{ is the family size of the } j^{th} \text{ household.} \qquad (7.9)$$

$$= (Z-1)\hat{n} + n_i = N_{z-i} + n_i, \text{ since households are identical.} \qquad (7.10)$$

The above re-writing is designed to set the stage for a Z-person prisoners' dilemma game.

Before turning to a specification of economic behaviour, we need a technical relationship between population size and the return on economic activity. Accordingly, let K stand for the size of the immediate environment that the village has access to, and Y for output. Then

$$Y \leq H(N,K) \qquad (7.11)$$

where $H(.)$ is a production function with constant returns to scale in two factors (that is, $H(\lambda N, \lambda K) = \lambda H(N,K)$ for $\lambda > 0$) with positive but diminishing returns to each factor. In addition, of course, $H(0,K) = 0$. Using the property of constant returns to scale,

$$H(N,K) = KH(N,1) = H(N,1) \text{ if } K \text{ is normalized and set equal to 1.} \qquad (7.12)$$

Write $H(N, 1) = F(N)$ for which it is assumed that:

$$F(0) = 0 \qquad \text{(that is, zero population means zero output)} \qquad (7.13)$$

$F'(N) > 0$ (population increase yields additional output)   (7.14)

$F''(N) < 0$ (marginal product decreases with population size since V, the local environment, is fixed in size)   (7.15)

$\lim_{N \to \infty} F(N) =$ a constant (output is bounded from above since K, the local environment, is fixed in size)   (7.16)

These assumptions imply that

$$\frac{F(N)}{N} > F'(N) \text{ and that } \lim_{N \to \infty} \frac{F(N)}{N} = 0 \qquad (7.17)$$

Note that $F(N)/N$ is the average output which decreases with N. Now let $n_i F(N)/N$ be the ith household's output given its size of n_i. Clearly, $n_i F(N)/N$ decreases with N. What it means is that if there was immigration into the area, $F(N)/N$ would fall and with it, every villager's output. In other words, population increase has an adverse external effect on existing production.

Normalize the price of a unit of output to 1 and denote by w the opportunity cost of labour. Assume that all households are price takers and profit maximizers. Let $y_i = n_i F(N)/N$ denote the output of the ith household. Then the profits of the ith household are given by:

$$\pi_i = y_i - wn_i = n_i \frac{F(N)}{N} - wn_i = n_i \frac{F(N_{z-i} + n_i)}{N_{z-i} + n_i} - wn_i$$

$$= n_i \frac{F((z-1)\hat{n} + n_i)}{(z-1)\hat{n} + n_i} - wn_i, \text{ using equation (7.10)} \qquad (7.18)$$

We now consider the ith household's choice of its family size. n_i is chosen to maximize π_i which implies the following condition:

$$\frac{F[(Z-1)\hat{n} + n_i]}{(Z-1)\hat{n} + n_i} + n_i \frac{F'[(Z-1)\hat{n} + n_i]}{(Z-1)\hat{n} + n_i} - n_i \frac{F[(Z-1)n + n_i]}{[(Z-1)n + n_i]^2} = w \quad (7.19)$$

Condition (7.19) must be satisfied for all i and since by symmetry $n_i = n$ for all i, it becomes:

$$\frac{F(\hat{N})}{\hat{N}} + \hat{n}\frac{F'(\hat{N})}{\hat{N}} - \hat{n}\frac{F(\hat{N})}{\hat{N}^2} - w = 0, \hat{N} = N\hat{n} \tag{7.20}$$

This may be re-expressed as:

$$\frac{F(\hat{N})}{\hat{N}} - \frac{1}{Z}\left\{\frac{F(\hat{N})}{\hat{N}} - F'(\hat{N})\right\} = w \tag{7.21}$$

The solution to equation (7.21) above, $\hat{N}$, may be referred to as free procreation equilibrium population.

Is there another outcome (that is, equilibrium population and profits) which is superior to the $(\hat{N}, \hat{\pi})$ outcome derived above? Suppose that somehow the villagers get together and act as a single body to manage their population. Assume that the body acts so as to maximize the total village profits. Anticipating the results, note that such maximization would take into account the population externality imposed by the villagers on each other. More formally, the body maximizes

$$F(Zn) - wZn \tag{7.22}$$

and then divides this aggregate profit equally between the villagers. The first order condition is:

$$F'(Z\tilde{n}) = w, \qquad Z\tilde{n} = \tilde{N} \tag{7.23}$$

where $\tilde{n}$ is the solution to equation (7.23).

Whereas $\hat{n}$ was referred to as free procreation equilibrium, $\tilde{n}$ can be referred to as the Pareto-efficient procreation equilibrium. We now show that $\hat{n} > \tilde{n}$. Equation (7.23) implies that $F'(\tilde{N}) - w = 0$ whereas equation (7.21) gives:

$$F'(\hat{N}) - w = \frac{(1-Z)}{Z}\left\{\frac{F(\hat{N})}{\hat{N}} - F'(\hat{N})\right\} < 0, \text{ (making use of 7.17)} \tag{7.24}$$

It follows that $F'(\tilde{N}) > F'(\hat{N})$, and given that $F''(N) < 0$, it also means that:

$$\hat{N} > \tilde{N} \quad \text{or} \quad \hat{n} > \tilde{n} \tag{7.25}$$

Clearly, under free procreation equilibrium, population size (and household size) is greater than that under Pareto-efficient equilibrium. Since $F'(\hat{N}) < w$ whereas $F'(\tilde{N}) = w$, it follows that

$$\hat{\pi} < \tilde{\pi} \tag{7.26}$$

In other words, by capturing the rent to the local natural resource, the villagers are less poor. It is in this sense of a higher standard of living that equation (7.25) states that at the free procreation equilibrium there is overpopulation.

A prisoner's dilemma interpretation
The above problem can be viewed as a prisoner's dilemma. In such a dilemma, the collective outcome of individual household decision making can, in logic, be improved upon. Consider a household deciding on the marginal child. If the given household decides 'to have the marginal child' (call this strategy D) and all the other households do not, then the pay-off to the given household is the best (highest). On the other hand, if it decides 'not to have the marginal child' (call this strategy C) and all the other households do, then the pay-off is the worst (lowest) – the household is a sucker. However, if the household gets smart and plays D and all the others play D as well then the pay-off is better but this is bettered by *everyone* playing C. It is this that gives rise to the possibility of improvement because, without any co-ordination, it is in each player's interest to play D no matter what the others are expected to play. It is a dilemma because everyone can be made better off by playing C although it is not obvious how that may be accomplished. Even if everyone agrees to play C, they have to discover a mechanism for enforcing this agreement.

In the rural third world prisoner's dilemma example we had assumed that the pay-off was in terms of profits. The collective outcome of unco-ordinated individual decision making in that situation was depressed profits. Of course there also resulted more children which leads one to ask: suppose the objective were to maximize the number of surviving children, would not then that outcome be the best? In fact, it turns out that because there are fewer resources per child, the children are undernourished and that adversely affects their survival chances. This, in fact, is the prisoner's dilemma problem that observers normally have in mind when being concerned about large family size. The collective outcome of the selfish individual goal of maximum number of children is environmental and resource decline so that people fail to achieve what they desire. Our goal of hereditary immortality has the inevitable conclusion of hereditary oblivion.

This dilemma can be motivated by thinking about jobs and unemployment. In the situation in which jobs are fixed by the technology of production and the wage rate cannot fall further, an increase in the number of children means that a given couple's marginal child has a smaller chance of getting a job. However, if everyone refrained from procreation then the given couple's marginal child would have a greater chance and the goal of having the maximum number of surviving children would be enhanced. Yet logic compels each couple to have many children in order to increase the chances of any one of its children getting a job. The above reasoning is simply a variation of the main argument in Chapter 6. There it was advanced that a couple in the third world goes for a large family in order to enhance the survival chances of its dynasty. Here we have drawn out the collective implication of each couple's thinking in that manner.

Our analysis of production inefficiency in the rural third world was over the short run. However these short-run inefficiencies can have a cumulative long-run effect of environmental degradation. Most obvious degradation is quantitative in the sense that the resource base shrinks – desertification, loss of forest cover and so on. Since the rural population is highly dependent on natural resources, the quantitative loss implies greater poverty. If so, this is interesting because of the debate: does poverty cause population growth or is it the other way round? Here, its clear that population growth causes poverty.

Environmental consequences of population increase can also have a qualitative dimension with far-reaching consequences and it is to these that we turn next.

7.8   Environment externalities

Our civilization has resulted from people's abilities to innovate and to create. Economists think that we are also particularly good at substituting for scarce materials and at developing solutions when need becomes apparent. But this is an incomplete picture of ourselves. We have been able to innovate within natural ecological systems which have the resilience to experience wide change and still maintain the integrity of their functions. However, the resilience of the natural systems is finite and it is thought that the present population, together with other factors, is stretching the limits of natural resilience (see Hollings, 1973, Hollings et al., 1994 and Perrings et al., 1994). As a consequence, the environment has become more vulnerable.

If so, we could be in a destablizing regime. Stability works on negative feedbacks, whereas positive feedbacks can cause the ecosystem to go into an eventual freefall. Here is an example of a positive feedback associated with population growth and environmental resilience. As human population increases, there is more exploitation causing loss of wild species and genetic biodiversity. This decreases resilience of natural eco-systems which, in turn, spurs human population growth as couples insure against loss of resilience by having more children. In this version of positive feedbacks, people are clearly caught in a prisoner's dilemma. People desire survival security yet their private actions to raise security yield a collective outcome in which security gets worse. Any given couple cannot unilaterally do something about this state of affairs since others are not likely to follow suit. The situation calls for collective action.

In fact, the whole earth may be caught in a prisoner's dilemma because of the emergence of planetary interconnections. Such connections are evidenced by the increase of greenhouse gases and the thinning of the ozone layer. An implication of such interconnections is that local action in one part of the globe has an effect on another, possibly distant, part of the globe. Furthermore, if natural resilience is in a decline, then such effects could have magnified implications.

It could be reasonably argued that the environmental consequences of population size are uncertain. However, if some of these possible consequences are also irreversible, then we could lose out on options. Of course, the value of such an option is difficult to determine and it also depends on our risk preferences.

7.9 Overcrowding and the spread of viruses
Overcrowding implies greater contact between people. Now, warm human bodies are potential hosts to viruses and greater contact means a greater probability of viruses spreading. Viruses normally die out of their own accord after they have run the full course but, with more people around it may be that more people are infected before the virus dies out. The reasoning is interesting: it is not in the interest of a potentially deadly virus to kill its host but, with more people, a virus can afford to have 'unfit' members who do kill the host and die with the host. So, much killing takes place before the virus ceases to be deadly.

If overcrowding is also accompanied by poverty and therefore squalor, bad sanitation and so on, then the risk of epidemics breaking out and spreading increases.

7.10 Conclusion
Our population growth has traced out a J curve thus far in our history. From hereon, there are three possibilities to consider: (1) a population die-back, just as in nature, and that would involve great human suffering; (2) an indefinite continuation of the J-curve, something that has never been observed in nature; and (3) the J-curve turning into a S-curve due either to carrying capacity/environmental constraints (as in nature) or overcrowding serving as surrogate prices inducing couples to self-regulate fertility or adopt deliberate collective action to reduce population growth such as price-based regulations, direct intervention from the centre and so on. Under (3) our standard of living could suffer and this chapter has focused on such welfare consequences.

A population size problem is a scale problem – there is presumed an optimum population size and the overpopulation problem gets worse the more the actual population exceeds the optimum. That happens because the adverse external effects worsen. The externalities that we have considered in this chapter are of a reciprocal kind which, together with underpriced resources, give rise to prisoner's dilemma situations. In the prisoner's dilemma situations that we have looked at, there is either waste of effort and resources or loss of welfare, and there is also the possibility of reducing waste or increasing welfare by reducing population size.

Prisoner's dilemma situations can persist. This is because although everyone realizes that they would all be better off with a smaller population size, they are unable to strike an implicit or explicit contract to that effect. The problem is of enforceability of such contracts. So, unilateral action by an individual household only makes matters worse for the household concerned. However, there is the possibility of success with collective action. The problem lies in converting the possibility into actuality and it is such policy matters that we address next.

8 Self-regulation of family size in a community

8.1 Introduction

This chapter looks at the problem of large family size. It is thought that overpopulation – 'too many people in too small an area' so that adverse externalities prevail – is with us and that it has to do with couples having too many children. It is also perceived that the tendency to have large families in certain parts of the world is persistent.

There is a biological tendency for human beings to procreate – we have tremendous sexual appetite which knows no seasons. Large families, therefore, should come as no surprise. On the other hand, we do observe that small families are also widespread. In fact, countries such as Norway, Switzerland, Canada and New Zealand appear to be sparsely populated (we ignore the intriguing question that these countries may be 'under-populated'). There are a number of possible reasons (for example, prosperity and shortage of suitable land for habitation) including that of self-regulation. While it is not too surprising to come across *individual* couples successfully practising voluntary birth control, it would be fascinating to find *societies* that successfully practise it. This needs examination.

Successful self-regulation of family size at the individual level indicates a triumph of rationality over biological urge. Successful self-regulation at the community level indicates the triumph of collective rationality. This would be quite amazing and we devote sections 8.7–8.11 to exploring this topic. To make our task analytically more focused we presume that the large family size problem is a prisoner's dilemma. (The problem need not necessarily always be a prisoner's dilemma, of course. Having large families can be a rational response to survival uncertainty or families can be 'locked in' the tradition of a large family.) Then the solution is analytically tractable.

The earlier sections of this chapter serve as a background to the large family size problem and possible solutions. The failure of existing solutions is seen as an 'institutional problem' (sections 8.2, 8.3). One school of thought is pessimistic about intervention (section 8.4), another advocates indirect intervention (section 8.5) while a third, (section 8.6), believes in direct intervention.

8.2 'Institutional arrangement' to regulate population in nature

In section 7.4 we reasoned that world food supply is likely to continue to increase in the near future (although there may be a problem of food distribution with supplies failing to reach some impoverished regions of the Earth). This appears analogous to making food available to animal populations in laboratory experiments in which populations grow with food supply. Interestingly, no institutional structure of any kind is imposed on the laboratory populations. They have no territories, for instance. Therefore, in the finite space of a laboratory container where there are no partitions between the breeding animals, the animals simply get themselves 'packed' together. They can move about in the container but it must be a miserable existence despite adequate food supply. We labelled the source of such possible misery adverse overcrowding externalities.

In section 3.5 we examined territoriality as living arrangements in nature and noted that breeding pairs of animals achieve greater reproductive success when they breed in a territory. Territorial dynasties also have a higher survival probability than non-territorial dynasties. We also noted that territories have a spatial dimension and since territories have to have a minimum size, there is an upper limit on the number of territories within the niche of a given species. If population size is determined by the number of territories, then the device of territoriality avoids overcrowding.

A territory is like a private property and rights to it are enforced. Male lions, for instance, regularly patrol territory boundary, marking it at strategic places to assert their rights. If an intruding lion challenges then rights are enforced by expelling the intruder, with violence if necessary. Since a territory is like a private property, there is no social externality; we can say that externalities are internalized. Since there is only one 'player' occupying a territory, a prisoner's dilemma situation does not arise either. It would therefore appear that within a territory an institution arrangement to regulate population exists in nature.

There are two qualifications. First, lion numbers within a territory can fluctuate. In times of prey scarcity, the pride size is usually small and in times of abundance it is large. However, even in times of plenty, overcrowding is absent. Second, there are floating members of a territorial species who do not possess territories. However, according to natural selection, these animals on average cannot be fit. The mechanism behind natural selection is that (a) nature compels many offspring but (b) competition in nature means that not all can occupy the limited number of territories – only the fittest manage to acquire and hold them. It also turns out that the size of floating populations is small.

Two remarks seem worth making. One is that, although there is competition for territories, usually (though not always) such competition is of a non-violent kind. This makes sense in terms of survival since any species that struggles violently for existence will eventually lose. Hence there are substitutes for violent competition. The conflict-resolution machinery includes ritual posturing, mutually recognized status, pecking orders and so on. We humans, of course, also abhor war, conflict and violence and we have rules and regulations to respect territorial rights and laws to protect private property. Unfortunately, often some of these either don't work or are costly to enforce. The second remark is that in nature territories are held by individuals or individual families. Thus each lion pride holds a territory: lion prides do not collectively hold a territory; there is no lion community. This is a crucial difference when comparing animal species with humans for there are instances where human communities hold territories. From communities (and nation states) to collective decision making – a unique human attribute – is a straightforward step.

8.3   Societal selection and human institutions

In human societies there appears to be the process of societal selection, corresponding to natural selection, and it works as follows. It is reasonable to assume that, in order to increase survival chances and have surviving children, human parents need jobs, education, access to medical services and housing all of which make up human territorial slots or niche-spaces. So, we could have a situation in which all households compete against each other for the limited number of such spaces in society, with the result that not all will hold such spaces. So, as in nature, there may exist a surplus population without niche-spaces. But unlike in nature, societal selection does not imply that the surplus will breed less and eventually die. In real human societies, the surplus population does survive and breed. Indeed, this is so to such an extent that, on average, a mother in the surplus population can have more surviving children than a mother who has a niche-space. How can this be? Suppose there is a resource which is a freely available public good, just as food was freely available in laboratory experiments. Examples are common property resources in third world rural areas and the welfare state in the West. Then the persistence of such freely available resources can easily lead to a large and persistently surviving, breeding, non-territorial population. The circumstances are such that the non-territorial population has no economic incentive to limit procreation since the costs of child rearing are shared by the society. However, if the outcome is overcrowding then the society at large experiences its external effects.

There is another significant way in which human and animal societies differ. We have other institution devices – especially markets and specialization – and ingenious artefacts (for example, skyscrapers and transport network for commuters) that enable packing more niche-spaces in a given space. As a result, each niche-space is spatially narrow, raising the spectre of overcrowding. Consider the institution of a market which, unlike a territory, ignores living space and so contributes to overcrowding. Markets facilitate exchange of goods at impersonal prices. This permits specialization so that a baker can specialize in baking bread and a tailor in making clothes. One can liken such professions to niches in nature and slots in a profession to territories in a niche. As a result, a tailoring profession has slots for a certain number of tailors. But markets have been remarkably successful in creating a great many professions as well as in creating wealth so that a great many slots in a great many professions can now be supported. Allied with human ingenuity at technical innovation, we have managed to 'pack' a great many people – professionals and others – in, say, cities with skyscrapers.

How is it that markets have ignored the spatial dimension that is associated with territories? Either the spatial dimension does not matter – people 'like' living in crowds – so that the low price for space is the optimal one, or the spatial dimension does matter but there is market failure such that price for space stays stuck at a low level. If the latter is the case then we could say that we need additional institution arrangements to correct for market failure. In other words, markets have dealt with the resource problem but not the externality problem.

Concerning specific institutions to contain overcrowding externalities associated with population size we have a choice of either institutions that deal with population size itself or those that deal with the consequences of population size. For example, suppose we think that population size causes environmental degradation in the third world. Then we could look at the institution of the family and hypothesize that the extended family lowers the cost of child rearing compared to a nuclear family. As a result, family size in the third world will be larger on average. One solution then is to raise the cost of child rearing by some institutional device, for example, subsidies, via the tax system, to childless women. Alternatively, we could look directly at environmental degradation and hypothesize that the market sends the wrong signals, leading to over-exploitation of the environment. Then, either artificial prices can be imposed so that the environment has a higher market cost, or a bureaucracy be installed to draw up, monitor and enforce regulations to preserve the environment. There is, of course, a spectrum of institutional devices in-between these extremes of market regulation and direct regulation.

8.4 Laissez-faire: do nothing

We have arrived at the following position. We think that there are serious persistent adverse externalities associated with population size. These externalities reduce human welfare. So our interest is in the reduction of either overcrowding or overcrowding externalities. In this matter we cannot appeal to a demographic (fertility) transition which, when complete, arrives at an overcrowded world with its attendant human suffering, misery and vulnerability. Our institutional arrangements have, so far, failed to organize human living arrangements such that human suffering is minimized. Some third world cities can be likened to breeding bottles of laboratory experiments and many third world rural populations suffer from hunger, malnutrition, disease and the like. The question then is: can human ingenuity devise institutions to carry out the task of minimizing externalities? If yes, then a natural supplementary question is: will human ingenuity, in fact, deliver?

A broad observation is in order. That human ingenuity can devise institutions (for example, universities, research departments in firms and government) to raise the supply of resources is not in doubt. The record is excellent. But the record of humans in devising institutions to deal with social problems is not good. We appear to have persistent wars, conflicts, social tension, poverty, unemployment and so on. We seem to have a tendency to get locked in situations, such as a prisoner's dilemma, which lead to losses in social welfare. So while we have a good record of increasing, say, food supply in step with population increases, we have a dismal record of containing the external effects of population size.

To rely on human ingenuity, which should accrue with population growth, to devise institutions to contain external effects of population size does not seem like a great idea. Perhaps we should concentrate on regulating population size itself. Even here, we are faced with a tricky question: will intervention improve matters or will it simply be a waste of resource or will it even make the situation worse?

There is a school of thought for which laissez-faire has become a religious belief. It believes that in the long run good order spontaneously results when things are left alone. Laissez-faire economists have an unshakeable belief in markets and trust the impersonal regulatory role of the price mechanism. They think that competition governed by the price mechanism implies that the interests of the individual and that of the society coincide. Thus, all that humans consciously need to do is to ensure that impediments (for instance, the obstruction that prevents the price of space rising when overcrowding threatens) to market forces are removed. Allied to the above belief is the tenet that once the allocation of goods and services is optimal, we can rely on technology and technical progress to raise prosperity. Concerning reasons (overcrowding externalities, poverty, environmental degradation and so on) given for intervention in the previous chapter, those advocating a laissez-faire stance might say that intervention would make these problems worse.

While 'nature knows best' hints at deep wisdom, we have the case that these population-related external effects are not only persistent, but also worsening. In fact, ecologists argue that 'nature knows best' is precisely the cause of overpopulation and the reason for low human welfare. It is a safe bet that this problem of low welfare is likely to persist, spread and worsen if nothing is done about it.

8.5 Indirect intervention: removing institutional constraints

There is another school of thought which acknowledges a population problem but which has an aversion to policies that directly attempt to reduce fertility rates. It upholds personal liberties, particularly in the sensitive arena of procreation. It also questions whether the benefits of a smaller population outweigh the costs of human pain and suffering as a result of direct intervention which restricts personal liberties. However, if the causes of overpopulation have to do with imperfections elsewhere in the economy (land monopolies, existence of a welfare state and so on), then there is scope for intervention to redress past policy mistakes: that is, break up land monopolies, dismantle the welfare state, and so on.

8.6   Indirect intervention: correct pricing of goods and services

It is somewhat unusual to consider institutional constraints (section 8.5) before incorrect pricing but the reason turns out to be a good one as we shall see. Consider the connection between overpopulation and the underpricing of firewood (Dasgupta, 1993). Firewood in the rural third world is a common property resource and, like most such resources, its price is zero. There is, of course, the opportunity cost of labour in collecting it but it is a task often assigned to children. They, by collecting fuel, acquire additional value. Therefore, market failure in firewood contributes to a large family size.

One would then have thought that an appropriate response to reducing family size would be for the government concerned to raise the price of firewood. It is here that the barriers of institutional constraints come in. Raising the price of firewood is bound to meet with political and social resistance and may also prove to be administratively costly.

8.7   Self-regulation

Self-regulation is attractive: there are no administrative costs and no bureaucracy. Of course, there is no need for outside intervention either. Some observers regard self-regulation with fervour and assert that it is the only conscious 'policy' that works in the long run. Examples of apparent self-regulation abound and it may have worked in the past.

We want to examine if couples can self-regulate family size. It will be presumed that there are conditions under which self-regulation of family size works and our task will be to uncover these conditions. We can then go on to examine if such conditions arise in practice. To make our task easier we will treat the family size problem as a prisoner's dilemma. This restricts any application of our analysis but it also brings sharper focus to the analysis.

Population problem as a prisoner's dilemma
Earlier, in Chapter 2, the micro-ecological model asserted that a couple wants the maximum number of children it can afford. There is survival uncertainty and the large-young gambit dictates a trade-off between family size and resources. This micro-ecological model was refined in Chapter 6 and it predicted a large family size. An underlying assumption was that of low child-rearing costs. A typical couple often does not bear the full costs of child rearing because there is access to a common property resource. A given couple's private decision to

have children will then impose social costs by inflicting an adverse effect on the common property resource; the resource gets to be 'overexploited' or 'stretched' so that there is not enough to go round to yield many healthy surviving children. As a result, the community may get locked in a prisoner's dilemma; everyone wants many surviving children but the collective outcome of such private decision making is that there are fewer surviving children per couple than in the case where people practise restraint in procreation and the resource does not get 'stretched'. The prisoner's dilemma is a non-zero sum game (chess is a zero sum game in which a win for one player is a loss for the other) in which the community can win since there is the common property resource handing out 'free' goods. (The classic reference to prisoner's dilemma is Rapoport, 1960). The way to victory is collusion or replacing competition with a co-operative agreement to restrict procreation.

The outcome of decision making in the micro-model of Chapter 5 can also give rise to a prisoner's dilemma situation. In that model, the utility function has child and adult services as arguments. If the utility of household also depends on congestion (the bigger the crowds the lower the utility), then the collective outcome of private decision making is a prisoner's dilemma situation.

Community and collective action
There is, in theory, a collective solution to the prisoner's dilemma problem. Since every family can be made better off by restricting family size, each family has voluntarily to agree to this decision and to abide by the agreement. The practical problem with such a solution is that there is a private incentive to break the contract which, in the absence of countervailing incentives, dominates. On the other hand, if the voluntary agreement is arrived at within the context of a community, then it is possible that the private incentive to renege on the contract can be subjugated to the private incentive to identify with the spirit of the community.

Community is a phenomenon within human society by which the identity of the individual becomes bound up with identification with the group. Community is learnt. The learning began when we were hunter-gatherers. Everyone knew everybody and there was general awareness of the nature of the community and the resources of the community itself. People had a good idea of what their commons could support. Also perceived was a need for a common obligation, (like control of population), for otherwise the community could destroy itself. A common obligation required some restraint on private self-seeking (see Ardrey, 1970, for the importance of this). The desire to identify with the community usually strongly supported most collective obligations.

In our analysis we shall assume the existence of a community. And, of course, we shall assume the existence of a prisoner's dilemma so that the possibility of making everyone better off exists.

8.8   How might co-operation in communities have arisen?

Co-operation in human societies has repeatedly been observed. How could it have arisen? Here is one possibility (the classic reference for co-operation in animals is Trivers, 1971).

1. (*Kinship* or genetic relatedness.) First of all we need to specify the way in which individuals with co-operative tendencies might happen to have clustered together so that they could all engage in a non-zero game, that is, benefit at the environment's expense. The way this is accomplished was that people were more likely to be living close to their relatives than to random members of the population.
2. (*Viscosity* or tendency for individuals to continue living close to their place of birth.) Through most of history, and in most parts of the world (the modern world might prove an exception though), most people have rarely strayed more than a few miles from their birthplace.
3. (*Local clusters.*) As a result, local clusters of genetic relatives tended to build up.
4. (*Similarity.*) Genetic relatives tend to be alike in both physical features and other respects (e.g. behaviour). For instance, they will share the genetic tendency to co-operate – or not to co-operate. So even if co-operation is rare in the population as a whole, it may still be locally common.
5. (*Repeated interaction.*) Obviously, in a local enclave, individuals with co-operative tendencies should meet each other often enough to have a stake in future encounters.
6. (*Anticipation.*) Humans, as distinct from other species, try to guess the future and to plan long term. Therefore, humans in local enclaves with co-operative tendencies will anticipate future encounters.
7. (*Co-operation.*) Community members will realize that such encounters can be made profitable by co-operation (see Gergen, Greenberg and Willis, 1980, who emphasize intangible benefits of such co-operation). If so, they will behave co-operatively, employing co-operative strategies.

To examine the sort of co-operative strategies which could be employed, and reasons for the persistence of such strategies, we need to introduce the notion of a supergame.

8.9   Supergames

A supergame (or a repeated game) is simply a sequence of one-shot games played through time. Whereas in a one-shot game players meet only once and the game is over after the first meeting, in a supergame players meet every period. When the players meet, they make their moves simultaneously, that is, in ignorance of the other player's choice. The novel feature of a supergame is that each player's move can be based on the observed history of past moves of the other players. Such moves are called conditional moves. Depending on the record of an opponent at hand, a player can either co-operate on the next move and thereby reward the opponent or not co-operate in order to punish.

Individual strategies – a strategy is now best thought of as a plan of action – can be quite intricate in a supergame and there can also be an infinite number of strategies. Therefore, in order to think clearly, it is useful to classify them into conditional and unconditional strategies (see the appendix to this chapter for examples of unconditional strategies). In the context of supergames, conditional strategies are more interesting because a player can base his current move on the past moves made by the other players.

Having introduced the notion of a supergame, we need to place it in an analytical framework that deals with the population problem. Therefore, consider a rural community of N members which satisfies the seven features of a co-operative community presented in the section above. We note that in every period the members of this small community interact with each other in a number of ways.

To introduce the population problem as a prisoner's dilemma problem into the analytical framework, assume that every couple prefers mutual restraint in procreation to no restraint; perhaps everyone realizes that there is no point in uncontrolled breeding if that reduces chances of having surviving children. But any couple would be best off not restraining at all when all the others are, provided it can continue to participate in other community activities.

8.10 Conditional strategies to enforce agreements

Assume that the participants in a community reach an agreement to practise restraint in procreation. Since everyone in the community knows each other and is in contact with each other, the agreement can be monitored. Concerning the problem of enforcing the agreement, it is precisely the difficulty of monitoring agreements (and also enforcing them) that normally accounts for the persistence of the prisoner's dilemma situation. However, in a supergame where conditional strategies are utilized, such difficulties may be resolved. One such strategy is the following:

Grim (or unforgiving)

a) Start by making the move of co-operation (including restraint of family size) in all aspects of community life.
b) Continue to play co-operation as long as others choose to do so in the previous constituent game.

c) However, if once any couple chooses non-restraint in family size, you at once switch to non-cooperation with it in all aspects of community life forever. But you continue to co-operate with the others in the community.

So the deviant is free to have a large family but is made an outcast. Those who stick to community co-operation simply exclude the couple from their circle. The deviant can even be expelled. It is this threat of the punishment of an outcast that usually does the trick of getting everyone to practise restraint in family size. As long as the threat is credible, it need not be carried out. As a result, the implicit agreement to restrain family size is simply enforced by the credible threat to withdraw social co-operation. It is in this sense that there is self-enforcement.

Grim is really a strategy of behaviour and is therefore a social norm or social convention. It is easy to show that the grim strategy combination is an equilibrium combination provided that subjective discount rates are 'not too high'. However, one shortcoming of grim is that the threatened punishment is too severe: it serves out eternal punishment to someone who lapses even once. So no mistakes are allowed. However, there is another conditional strategy that gives second chances to even those who deliberately attempt to take advantage of the public good of co-operation.

Tit for tat strategy (or co-operate with your opponent if it co-operates with you)
Consider the following strategy:

a) Start the game by co-operating.
b) Thereafter, in period t choose the move that the others choose in period $t-1$. (That is, in every subsequent move copy the previous move made by the others.)
c) Once, any couple chooses not to restrain in procreation, you switch to non-co-operation in all community activities with it for one period. You continue community co-operation with others.

Comparing tit for tat (TfT) with grim, in both you co-operate at the starting date. Also in both you reciprocate co-operation. However, whereas in grim once a couple does not co-operate it is rendered an outcast forever, in TfT you retaliate as soon as it does not co-operate but forgive it as soon as it reverts to co-operation. This difference can be stated in an alternative way: in grim you co-operate with a couple if it has always co-operated in the past without a single lapse whereas in TfT you co-operate if it has co-operated in the previous move, irrespective of the history of its distant past.

TfT has many interesting and commendable features. (a) *Brave*. One feature is that you are prepared to co-operate in advance of any evidence that others will respond with co-operation. You risk exploitation in the first move. (In fact any strategy which co-operates with itself, and TfT is such a strategy, carries this risk of initial exploitation.) (b) *Nice*. TfT is never the first to defect. It is capable of defection (or non-co-operation) but it does so only in retaliation. (Nasty strategies defect even when not provoked.) (c) *Tough*. TfT punishes non-co-operation by defecting in the next move. (d) *Forgiving*. TfT has a short memory. It raps a defector over the knuckles instantly but, after that, lets bygones be bygones. It rewards good behaviour by co-operating the next time. This property helps to damp down what might become long and damaging runs of mutual recrimination.

If your opponent plays TfT, should you? That is, is your response of TfT to your advantage or can you do better by employing some other strategy? If the discount factor (that is, your preference for future consumption vis à vis present consumption) is not too large then its worth responding with TfT (see appendix). In other words, it is worth playing TfT if people are not unduly myopic. It is also easy to show that if the discount factor condition is satisfied then the (TfT, TfT) strategy combination is an equilibrium combination (see Axelrod, 1987, for social applications of TfT).

Properties of TfT

TfT has great appeal (see Axelrod (1984) who has championed TfT). In part, this may be due to its simplicity. It should also be easy to practise. However, it has two awkward features. One is that it is not evolutionary stable. An evolutionary stable strategy is defined as a strategy which, if most members of a population adopt it, cannot be bettered by an alternative strategy. An evolutionary stable strategy is a strategy that does well against copies of itself. The rationale for this is as follows. A successful strategy is one that dominates the population. Therefore, it will tend to encounter copies of itself and it will not be successful unless it does well against copies of itself.

So an evolutionary stable strategy is one which carried on doing well when it is already numerous in the population of strategies. It must not be invadable, when it is already common in a population, by another strategy. TfT is not evolutionary stable, that is, a (TfT,TfT) strategy combination can be taken over by other strategy combinations. Whereas TfT cannot be invaded by a nasty strategy such as 'always defect' (this is because TfT is tough – it retaliates), invasion by another nice strategy is a different matter because in a population of nice strategies they all look alike and behave exactly like one another: they all co-operate all the time. So another nice strategy such as 'always co-operate' can drift into a community practising TfT without being noticed. This matters because unlike TfT, 'always co-operate' is not stable against invasion by nasty strategies such as 'always defect' as it does not retaliate.

The second awkward problem is that TfT does not make use of the entire history or reputation of a player when meting out punishment, this cannot be sensible in a community where people have known each other for a considerable period of time. But it is relatively easy to modify TfT to take account of reputation. Consider, therefore, the following version.

Tit for two tats (Tf2T)

a) In the first period start by co-operating in all aspects of community life.
b) Continue to co-operate as long as others chose to do so in the previous move.
c) If anyone chooses not to restrain, you allow two such defections in a row before retaliating.

Tf2T therefore gives a second chance so that it is more likely to be practised by long-standing friends than TfT. It probably better reflects what communities might do in practice: give second chances, test out new members, condone cases of hardship, not render repentant characters outcast and so on. Tf2T (or f3 or 4 or 5... for that matter) appears to be a strong candidate for a strategy that communities might practise.

Co-operation in practice
When thinking about a community whose members employ co-operative strategies, one is thinking about the way in which behaviour in the community is characterized. TfT or Tf2T is then a community behavioural trait. Since people in the community follow the trait one could call it a community norm or a social norm. We can think of a social norm as a behavioural convention that is followed in a mechanical manner, involving little conscious effort. It means that people in a community respond to each other's strategy as a matter of routine. If people in a well-defined group routinely practise TfT for instance then we could also call TfT a cultural trait of that group.

Growth of co-operation
We have set out conditions that encourage little enclaves of co-operation to come into existence. Once established, these local clusters can grow. Suppose there is a large population in which there is not much movement so that individuals tend to resemble their immediate neighbours more than their more distant neighbours. The immediate neighbours, observing correlation between co-operative traits and prosperity, in a co-operative enclave, will wish to join the club. Insiders may encourage them to join, perceiving economies of scale such as a large contact network. Alternatively, the neighbours may simply copy the traits.

    For how long can a club survive? If a cultural trait is not evolutionary stable then it may be invaded. Here is an example of how a TfT strategy pair can be invaded. Suppose there are two players engaged in a supergame and that both are employing TfT strategy. Now suppose that one player changes his strategy to 'always co-operate'. Then the other player can also switch to 'always co-operate' and be just as successful. Neither player is any worse off. This means that an equilibrium strategy such as TfT may be invaded by a mutant strategy 'always co-operate'.

8.11 Breakdown of self-regulation

'Always co-operate' can survive in a friendly population but not in a hostile one. It can invade TfT but that does not matter for co-operation as long as the population remains friendly. If, however, the population changes to a hostile one 'always co-operate' can be invaded by a nasty strategy, such as 'always defect'.

Here is an example of population change and invasion. Suppose there is a community that has implicit rights to its local resource. The community has a stable population composition and its members have low subjective discount rates. With an eye to the future, the community restrains from overexploiting the local resource and family size is regulated. Now suppose that due to population growth in the country at large, there is immigration into the area and the immigrants, who have no stake in the community, are not interested in co-operation. If the residents continue to practise 'always co-operate' then they lose out (they conserve the resource and practise family size restraint) whereas the immigrants gain (they exploit the resource so as to support larger family sizes). One by one, the residents have to 'join the party' if they are to survive. Had the residents practised TfT, which is tough, they would have retaliated by expelling the immigrants after having found out their intention to rip-off the local community.

However, co-operation in a community practising TfT can break down if the environment changes so as to raise subjective discount rates. An example is a failure of rains that ushers in a famine. The rate of resource exploitation in relation to population size then becomes unbalanced until the rate of exploitation is stepped up, at least by those who are the poorest members of the community. Co-operation is then threatened – members with low discount rates retaliate by rendering the others as outcasts. However, if the famine is short-lived and the defectors make amends then they are forgiven and co-operation is restored.

Over the years, we have witnessed an erosion of social norms that encourage co-operation. The fundamental reason is rapid change in the environment caused by technological advances, population growth itself, globalization and so on. Specific changes have been migration, development in communications linking isolated communities to the rest of the world, resettlement programmes, predatory governments (Zaire for example), unscrupulous wealthy classes (Brazil for example) and widening inequality. Such changes serve to repeatedly alter the composition of communities and also weaken the implicit community rights to the local resource. In a mobile, fluid society, co-operation and hence self-regulation of the type we have been analysing has little chance of getting a foothold – conditions are no longer favourable. Boulding's thoughts (Boulding, 1977) are pertinent here. He believes that a small, stable community gives identity to individual members and inoculates the 'habit of subordination'. Roughly translated, it means that a community needs to have a slowly evolving history and the incentives to co-operate. If you remove either the history or the conditions that give rise to co-operation then self-regulation collapses at the community level (see also Cosmides and Tooby, 1989, who argue that cheaters cannot get away in a small community).

8.12   Conclusion

The background to this chapter has been the problem of population size (as opposed to population growth). It is, of course, presumed that there is an overpopulation problem, a view not shared by everyone. The presumption rests on the observation of persistent and pervasive externalities associated with population size. However, there is disagreement about relating the observed externalities to population size; the chances of technical change alleviating the external effects; people's capabilities of adapting to living in crowded environments; the magnitude of the beneficial externalities associated with human population size, for example, more people means greater human ingenuity; and so on.

The school of thought that we have been concerned with in this chapter believes that only self-regulation works in the long run. Moreover, self-regulation is economical in use of resources, for example, no bureaucracy is required. As a result, the only sort of intervention that is justified is that which creates conditions for spontaneous self-regulation to arise and persist. Accordingly, this chapter has analysed the conditions that are required for co-operative repeated games to take place. The reason for focusing on such games is that if we view the family size problem as a one-shot prisoner's dilemma then a repeated prisoner's dilemma game is a solution to the one-shot problem. A repeated game is really self-regulation in which participants simply adopt co-operative strategies.

It turns out that although conditions for such self-regulation were in place in the past, they are rapidly being replaced. The reasons for this erosion have to do with the rapid change taking place in the world at large. Essentially, for repeated games you need stable communities for which fast and frequent change is not conducive. In addition, if we are truly becoming a global economy, then the prisoner's dilemma is likely to get worse and the chances of spontaneous self-regulation less. Clearly, we need to explore other options.

Suppose, then, that there is a real overpopulation problem. What are the options available to us for dealing with the problem? There is a school of thought (the neo-Malthusians) which advocates direct intervention, meaning providing incentives to promote birth control and family planning. A variation is to provide subsidies to childless women, issue tradeable permits and so on (this is the subject of Chapter 10). Another option is indirect intervention – it may be that the price mechanism is potentially capable of the task of regulating population size except that it is impeded by imperfections in the economy. Removal of such impediments then is in order (see Chapter 9).

Appendix

Unconditional strategies

Unconditional co-operation (or always co-operate)   In this strategy, C (or co-operation) is played in every game irrespective of the opponent's moves. Call this indiscriminate co-operation. This strategy cannot be an equilibrium strategy for either player can obtain a greater pay-off by switching unilaterally to playing D (or defect) in every round. If you know that your opponent is going to play C whatever you do, you can do better by playing D.

Unconditional defect (or always defect)   Here D is played in every game irrespective of the opponent's moves. If both players play unconditional defect then it never pays either player to change his strategy unilaterally. (If a player were to play C in any of the constituent games he would get less than he would have done had he stuck to D.) As a result, mutual unconditional D in every move is always an equilibrium.

Conditional strategies
That mutual unconditional D strategy combination is an equilibrium in a prisoner's dilemma supergame is not an appealing result. After all, mutual defection is an equilibrium outcome in a one-shot prisoner's dilemma. However, it turns out that this equilibrium is not the only one. There are other equilibria and these can sustain mutual co-operation throughout a supergame. They concern conditional strategies and we have noted that tit for tat (or co-operate with your opponent if it co-operates with you) is one such strategy. Variations of TfT also result in equilibrium outcomes. Tf2T is one such variation: whereas in TfT you retaliate once your opponent defects, in Tf2T you allow two defections in a row before retaliating. Another variation is Naive Prober. This is basically identical to TfT except that, once in a while in a sequence of C moves, a D move is randomly thrown in.

Conditions under which (TfT, TfT) is an equilibrium combination
Here is the derivation of the condition under which it pays you to respond with TfT instead of unconditional D (the condition is easily generalized to encompass other strategies besides unconditional D):

1. If your opponent plays TfT and you play TfT as well then your pay-off is V in all periods and the discounted value of this sum is:

   $V\delta + V\delta^2 + V\delta^3 + ... = V(\delta/1 - \delta)$ δ is the discount factor

   $\delta = (1/1 + r)$, r is the discount factor

2. If your opponent starts by playing TfT and you respond with unconditional D then your initial pay-off is U instead of V and, in subsequent periods, Y instead of v, $U > V > Y$. So you gain initially, but lose out in all subsequent periods. The discounted value is

   $U\delta + (Y\delta^2 + Y\delta^3 + ...) = U\delta + \delta(Y\delta + Y\delta^2 + ...) = U\delta + y\delta(\delta/1 - \delta)$

3. So it is worth sticking to TfT if

   $V(\delta/1 - \delta) > U\delta + Y(\delta^2/1 - \delta)$ or, upon rearranging,

   $\delta > (U - Y)/(U - V)$

Therefore, if unilateral defection from TfT to unconditional D is not to pay, the discount factor must not be too small or, equivalently, the discount rate r must not be too great. As can be seen, how great depends on the constituent game pay-offs. In particular, the smaller the 'instant' gain from defection, $(U - Y)$, the less likely, other things being equal, will unilateral defection to unconditional D yield a gain in the supergame.

So, if the above condition is satisfied then the strategy combination (TfT, TfT) is robust against unilateral defection to unconditional D. However, if defection to unconditional D does not pay, might it nevertheless pay to defect to some other strategy? After all, there is an infinite number of other strategies from which to choose. But, it turns out, it can be shown that a necessary and sufficient condition for (TfT, TfT) to be an equilibrium is that each player's discount factor δ is no less than the larger of $(U - Y)/(U - V)$ and $(U - Y)/(Y - Z)$ i.e. $\delta > \max [(U - Y)/(U - V), (U - Y)/(Y - Z)]$, $U > V > Y > Z$. (At an equilibrium each player's strategy is the 'best response' to the other player's strategy in the sense that there is no strategy which would be better than the equilibrium strategy, given that the other player will use his equilibrium strategy.)

Of course, the above result does not imply that when the discount factor condition is satisfied, then (TfT, TfT) combination will actually be the outcome of the game. (Unconditional D, Unconditional D), for instance is also an equilibrium combination and the actual outcome can be any one of the equilibria.

9   Indirect intervention

9.1   Introduction

In Chapter 7 we argued that overcrowding resulting from overpopulation is the principal problem and in Chapter 8 we considered self-regulation as a mechanism for containing population size. Self-regulation is attractive because it is voluntary: it is not imposed on a community of economic agents by some external authority. Self-regulation requires that members of a community perceive gains in self-restraint that more than compensate for losses. As a consequence, it is welfare-improving. There is also the belief that the only form of regulation that ever works in the long run is, indeed, self-regulation since other forms of regulation are imperfect, inelegant, have unacceptable bureaucratic and administrative costs, suffer from incentive problems, and so on. However, as we have seen, successful self-regulation of family size at the local level requires certain favourable conditions which appear unlikely to be realized in practice today. In particular, unfettered population growth in the country at large contributes to a breakdown of local self-regulation. For instance, population growth elsewhere in a country ushers immigrants into a community and disturbs the conditions conducive to self-regulation.

It follows that one of the pre-conditions for successful self-regulation at community level is a reduction in population growth, and therefore a reduction in the average family size, at country level. In this context, it is interesting to note that in most industrialized and newly developed economies, family sizes are small. There is a widespread impression that birth rates do appear to go down with a rise in economic prosperity. Perhaps economic development might turn out to be a solution to the problem of large family size in the third world countries.

Therefore, in this chapter, we resurrect the theory of the demographic transition introduced in Chapter 4. This theory is highly attractive for two reasons. First, it says that economic development reduces both poverty and population growth, hence it is a win–win situation. Second, direct regulation of population growth is not involved. The hard issue confronting the theory, however, is that of regulation of a country's population size; a country can eventually have a large population of many small families and that, as we have seen in Chapter 7, has some serious adverse external effects.

Essentially, this chapter reviews the economic growth and the demographic experience of Western Europe, Taiwan and South Korea, and Brazil and Mexico – in that order. The idea is to see what lessons can be drawn from the experience of these countries and also if the order in which countries become prosperous matters. In addition, we need to know how prosperity can be engineered for countries that are 'in the queue' and, accordingly, the second half of this chapter concentrates on one device that promises prosperity, a reduction in environmental degradation and a decline in fertility.

9.2   Cycles and technical progress

The ecological view on population has emphasized that population growth is related to cycles in food surplus. To restate, there is the ancient breeding goal to have the maximum number of surviving children. This implies that, with a resource constraint on population size and an inappropriate institutional arrangement, the masses occupy narrow niche-spaces. However, in due course, human ingenuity at tapping technical potential manages to convert the environment further into more material resources. With these extra resources, we create more niche-spaces for more families until the surplus resources are exhausted. And so on and on, the cycles recur (George, 1977).

As a prelude to the view that Europe's demographic transition signals a break from the cycle, consider recent European history. Until about 1800 British history was characterized by cycles. With every increase in Britain's population, food and land prices rose while wages stagnated (Wrigley and Schofield, 1981; Bengtsson 1992). Consequently, the standard of living fell for the masses. These features were echoed in other parts of Western Europe. Then, early in the nineteenth century, a technical revolution in agriculture occurred leading to a food surplus. The change was such that a smaller proportion of the population was required to work in the agricultural sector. At the same time, the industrial sector grew fast and absorbed more workers. Not surprisingly, the living standard of the masses rose in Britain. Other countries of Western Europe, as well as North America and Japan, followed this path of modern economic growth in the second half of the nineteenth century.

Uncertainty and modern economic growth

For the masses in the pre-industrial society, there was a great deal of uncertainty regarding access to food since harvests fluctuated. There was also uncertainty concerning access to fuel whenever winters were severely cold. Another element of uncertainty concerned the supply of land: tenancies could be terminated and altered, and even the peasant-proprietor could lose his holding. The final element of uncertainty concerned security in old age. All these components of uncertainty were reduced when living standards began their inexorable rise with the revolution in agriculture followed by the Industrial Revolution.

9.3   The mechanisms responsible for Europe's demographic transition

By demographic transition it is meant transition to lower fertility. This can be translated as a transition from large to small families. The underlying force propelling the demographic transition in Britain, Germany, Sweden and a few other western economies appears to have been technical progress. Consequently, as we have seen, the revolution in agriculture and the Industrial Revolution that followed led to rising living standards.

There were two institutional changes accompanying the fertility decline. One was that families became nuclearized. The other was that people organized themselves to live in urban areas. Even today, the landscape of tiny Britain with nearly 60 million people is largely empty spaces (farms, fields, woodland and so on) heavily dotted with urban areas. People are not spaced out; instead they live and work in clusters of overcrowded areas.

It is possible that the fertility decline may actually have been due to the processes of urbanization and nuclearization. Consider the five mechanisms linked to these processes and which are thought to have been conducive to small family size. One is child-rearing costs. Non-agricultural jobs in the urban area required a skilled labour force and that meant couples educating their children more. As we analysed in Chapter 5, couples who invest more in the human capital of their children tend to have fewer of them. Second, the expanding labour market in urban areas also ushered in work opportunities for women. Once again, as we analysed in Chapter 5, women whose market wages rise tend to have fewer children. Turning to the third mechanism, which is the collective consequence of micro-economic decision making, urbanization is associated with overcrowding and the associated overcrowding externalities may have served as a surrogate price thereby inducing a smaller family. For example, in a crowded environment the welfare of a large family decreases as the quality of life for each family member drops. Then, at the margin, fertility should decline.

The fourth mechanism lies outside the micro model of Chapter 5 which was constructed under the assumption of certainty. The expectation of a secure urban job increased economic security, reducing the dependence of parents on children for old age support and thereby reducing the economic benefits of children. Since survival chances of children were also perceived to increase, dynastic survival appeared to be more secure. According to the micro model of Chapter 6, this imparts a small family bias.

The final factor, independent of urbanization and nuclearization, in reducing family size was a 'taste' change. With technical progress, we had a wider range of permanent artefacts that serve to store our works of art and scientific discoveries for posterity. Once it dawned that there were substitutes for hereditary immortality, some of us went for the new vehicles.

Two comments are worth making. A single static micro model is not adequate in explaining fertility decline. The reasons are: comparative statics analysis does not capture the full richness of a dynamic phenomenon like fertility decline; the conventional micro model of Chapter 5 also ignores collective feedbacks; and, finally, so many factors must have been at play over the long-time period under consideration that the entire models themselves changed (for example, from micro-ecological to micro-economic).

While living standards have risen and fertility declined in Western Europe, the demographic transition has not been complete. As a result, population has increased, albeit slowly, so that there are now many more smaller families in Europe. In addition, the rise in living standards has really been a rise in material living standards accompanied by a decrease in the quantity and quality of the natural environment. Prosperity has also been accompanied by intra-country inequality.

An ecological interpretation of fertility decline
Is the observed phenomenon of the demographic transition consistent with an ecological explanation of family size, population growth and living standards? Briefly, according to ecological thinking, an increase in resources (resulting from some exogenous change such as technical progress) combined with the ancient breeding goal to maximize the number of surviving children leads to (a) population growth which, in turn, leads to (b) overcrowding externalities and eventually to (c) the masses living in narrow niche-spaces. (d) There is an air of inevitability about ecological thinking such that one can sense that the resulting outcome is Pareto-inferior in relation to some economic welfare criterion. It would appear that prediction (a) has been borne out – population in most western economies has grown and is expected to continue to grow. However, the growth rates have fallen. But noting the fast population growth rates when modern economic growth took off, the Western European population curves bear close resemblance to the S-curve predicted by ecologists. As for prediction (b) one could say Europe is overcrowded in the sense that population densities are high. However, opinion is divided on the associated externalities. Turning to prediction (c), it is evident that the spatial dimension to living space has been considerably reduced in urban areas and to this extent the masses can be described as living in narrow niche-spaces. On the other hand, material living standards have risen, people also live longer and healthier lives and are more economically secure than in the past. (d) Welfare is debateable. The mechanism that releases extra welfare with a smaller population is the reduction in external effects, such reduction more than compensating for the welfare loss due to a decrease in family size plus reduction in any positive externalities. For instance, while cities in the West exhibit many of the adverse externalities, many people find city-life stimulating and it is also thought that cities have propelled advances in arts and science.

On balance one could say that while the positive predictions of ecological thinking have been borne out, one has to reserve judgement on the normative prediction. Thus there is not much of a difference in the trend predictions of demographic transition theory and ecological thinking. The theories could be differentiated in their predictions if we could say something decisive about welfare. They could also be differentiated if we could check out a key assumption of ecological thinking: couples opt for the maximum number of children that they can afford. If it could be demonstrated that economic development leads to lower fertility because people choose to substitute parental consumption for children – the central tenet of Chapter 5 – then that would cast serious doubt on ecological thinking. Parental consumption can include using leisure time to create works of art or to make scientific discoveries in the expectation that these will be remembered forever. Such endeavours could serve as a substitute for hereditary immortality. Of course, they are better carried out by people who are free from poverty and have ample leisure time.

Armed with this background, we now turn to an application of demographic transition to two newly industralized countries of the Far East, namely Taiwan and South Korea, and two fast developing countries of South America, namely Brazil and Mexico. The two-pronged question is, as ever, is prosperity reducing fertility at household level and is the collective outcome attractive in terms of economic welfare?

9.4 Fertility transition in Taiwan and Korea

In the early 1950s, fertility started falling in Taiwan and, a decade later, also in South Korea. In both countries, fertility currently is a shade below the replacement rate. In addition to these two Far Eastern countries, Thailand, Malaysia and Indonesia have also experienced significant fertility declines in recent years (see Hetaseram and Roumasset, 1992, World Bank, 1993).

To begin with, as was the case with Western Europe, in both Taiwan and South Korea there was an improvement in agricultural productivity. This was due to serious land and capital market reforms undertaken in the 1950s which laid the basis for successful small-scale peasant agricultural production. This development meant that neither government had to contend with powerful landed-interest groups. As a result, prior to economic growth take-off, there was an extraordinary equal distribution of income and wealth. Another initial condition present was that of a skilled labour force relative to capital stock and income level.

Given these two initial conditions, in the early 1960s and thereafter, the Taiwanese and the Korean governments managed to engineer a significant increase in the private return to capital. They did so not only by removing a number of impediments to investment and establishing a sound investment climate but also by alleviating a co-ordination failure which had previously blocked economic take-off. The latter required a range of strategic interventions including investment subsidies, administrative guidance, and the use of public enterprise, most notably universal access to education and health.

The economic performance of Taiwan and Korea has come to be characterized as 'economic growth with equity'. Their economic growth continued into the

1990s and the growth rates were spectacular. Average living standards were substantially improved and fertility rates fell. Why did the pervasive state intervention not lead to bureaucratic rent-seeking and thereby defeat the objectives of the policy makers? The reason appears to be the relatively equal distribution of income. Furthermore, it may have been the case that by going full-out for growth, the bureaucracy believed that it would also share in the riches to come.

Comparing the experience of this Far Eastern duo with that of Western Europe after the Industrial Revolution, there are three notable differences. One is that of the initial conditions of equality and of skilled labour (See Oshima, 1992). The second is the active role of the government to promote 'growth with equity'. The third is the relatively much faster economic and demographic transition. The first two differences should help explain why so many other developing countries have failed with government interventions.

As in the case of Western Europe, urbanization appears to be primarily responsible for fertility decline. Urban jobs meant greater investment in human capital, raising child-rearing costs. Availability of urban jobs for women also raised the wife's opportunity cost. With greater job security, the insurance benefits of children fell. Finally, urbanization also meant overcrowding externalities serving as a surrogate price of large families.

As for the nomative question, it is undeniable that the mass of the people in Taiwan and South Korea are free from poverty although they do live in crowded urban areas. The people are healthier and live longer. To this extent they are certainly better off. Whether they are happier depends on the price paid for the higher living standard. Prosperity has been accompanied by overcrowding but we have no idea of the magnitude of the externalities associated with it. Prosperity has also been accompanied by an institutional change, the extended family making way for the nuclear family, and again we have only anecdotal evidence that this has led to a less happy society. Finally, there has been a reduction in the natural environment of the two countries. While this does not matter for the prosperity of these two trading countries – they can specialize in production, import food and raw materials, and the people can take holidays to countries with large areas of wilderness – it does have implications for countries that are lagging behind in the race for industrialization. Is the prosperity and fertility decline of Taiwan and South Korea at the expense of the third world countries in the sense that global inequality in living standards is necessary for the prosperity of the rich nations of the world?

9.5 Fertility transition in Brazil and Mexico

Possibilities of fertility transition may be discerned in the experience of Brazil and Mexico over the period 1960–90. In Brazil, and with a lag in Mexico, land in rural areas was consolidated into larger holdings which led to mass conversion of tenant farmers into wage labourers and also to large scale migration to urban areas. Just as it happened during the revolution in agriculture in Western Europe, the proportion of population in rural areas fell as a result of which, by 1980, two-thirds of the population was urban. However, there was also a significant difference from the European experience; in Brazil and Mexico the start of the fertility decline preceded the mortality decline: in the early 1960s, the number of children per family fell and in the late 1960s mortality substantially declined.

Overall, there was a modest increase in living standards although economic growth in each of two countries was far from steady. Unlike in Europe, income inequality also widened. By the early 1990s, parts of the urban sector in each of the two countries had become very modern and a growing number of people connected with this sector had a living standard similar to their counterparts in Western Europe. However, there was also substantial and growing urban poverty alongside sizeable rural poverty.

In attempting to analyse the experience of Brazil and Mexico, it is not easy to make the causal link between economic growth and fertility transition. There is the puzzling feature that both the urban rich and the urban poor have small families. It appears that it is urbanization and therefore overcrowding which was primarily responsible for the fertility decline and two of the mechanisms linked with urbanization, alluded to in the experience of both Western Europe and Taiwan and South Korea, appear to have been operative. With urbanization went human capital necessary to work in non-agricultural jobs and also market wage opportunities for women so that child rearing costs increased. Again, with urbanization, there was the expectation of securing a permanent job, raising the level of economic security and reducing the dependence on children for income support. A contributory factor here may have been the necessity of breaking up families given a spatial distribution of job opportunities.

9.6 Indirect intervention

The experience of several of the Far Eastern countries suggests that broad-based economic growth may well be sufficient to reduce fertility rates, if not necessary (urbanization and nuclearization may reduce fertility independent of growth). Broad-based growth also reduces poverty and inequality, of course. Such growth requires the economy to be well managed.

One example of bad management is managing the economy for the benefit of various interest and elite groups: urban consumers (as in Ethiopia), civil servants (as in India), land monopolies (as in Brazil) and so forth. Good management includes strengthening the agricultural sector. That means removing the imperfections in the rural capital and credit markets, lowering the exchange rate to increase agricultural exports, and breaking up land monopolies.

There is, in fact, a well-defined school of thought that relates broad-based prosperity, good management, land monopolies and fertility and the reasoning is as follows. To engineer broad-based prosperity, breaking up land monopolies (which is good management) should eventually precipitate fertility decline. So the key to fertility reduction (and, it also happens, environmental conservation) in Latin America, Africa and parts of Asia is an elimination of land monopolies. Let us turn to the Georgists.

The original thesis of George

Henry George (1839–97) was an American philosopher-economist best known for his book, *Progress and Poverty* (George, 1962). He thought that institutional arrangements are responsible for a great deal of poverty and misery. He was thinking specifically of private property rights to land being concentrated in the hands of a few. His argument was that land is indispensable for all human activities and if some own land and others are landless – he observed only a tiny minority owning land and the vast majority being landless – then this monopolistic distortion impedes the working of markets. As a result, there is considerable poverty and, of course, inequality. George was a social reformer in the sense that he wanted a change in institutional arrangements so as to reduce poverty, and he advocated removal of impediments to the operation of the markets. Specifically, he called for elimination of land monopoly to reduce involuntary poverty.

George's early US observations on the land and the poverty problem are echoed currently in many countries of South America, Africa and Asia. For the first illustration consider Brazil. It appears that as much as three-fifths of Brazil's arable acreage is covered by huge *latifundios* (or very large estates) controlled by a tiny minority. It is thought that half of these are idle, held for speculative purposes. Another large chunk is simply pastureland. It was estimated in the 1960s that 'total factor productivity on family farms was twice as high as on the large latifundio tracts of land' (Todaro, 1989). It was at this time that Brazil's military government embarked on resettling landless people in Amazon forests. The point is this: the practice of large rural families and the environment damage to Amazonia may be attributed to the existence of vested interests in land. A Georgist would argue that land resettlement was an inappropriate policy and what was needed instead was land redistribution.

The second illustration comes from the Philippines. Once again, a tiny minority owns the vast majority of land holdings. Consequently, in this agrarian society, the poor rural majority competes for a limited land resource. It is thought that this constrains the management of whatever land the poor farmers have. To make makers worse, the agrarian policy over the last several decades has promoted land resettlement rather than redistribution. Landless peasants have been encouraged to move to designated resettlement areas. The events in Palawan, the country's largest province, illustrate the adverse environment consequences. Incoming farmers, not accustomed to methods of growing food in forests, cleared and abandoned vast tracts of forests. The indigenous people of Palawan, who had developed sustainable agricultural practices, had to move to the hills in the interior since their land rights were not protected. Here, on the steep slopes, they had to farm more intensively in order to extract enough food to meet their subsistence needs. Unfortunately, this practice greatly reduced the fertility of the land. Once again, poverty and environmental degradation is attributable to the monopolistic elements in land holdings, not to population growth and once again Georgists would argue that land resettlement should have been replaced with land redistribution.

The third illustration is from Kenya. In 1972, it was recorded that the distribution of land in Kenya was highly skewed. About 0.1 per cent of landowners owned land made up of holdings that averaged 714 hectares in size, while 96 per cent of the landowners had holdings that were on average 3.8 hectares. So 1500 owners occupied 1.1 million hectares while 1.3 million households occupied 5 million hectares. Over the years soil erosion, land productivity decline and land fertility decline have become widespread and these are attributable to the skewed land distribution since this implies a skewed distribution of life–supporting resources which in turn means that the rural majority have to over-work their holding to meet subsistence needs. Poverty, of course, is widespread in rural Kenya.

The mechanism for fertility decline

The Georgist connection between a skewed distribution of land and population growth is poverty which is the same connection featured in the theory behind the demographic transition. The Georgist twist is that poverty is a result of skewed land distribution. This is of particular relevance to third world rural population where land is a direct life-support so that access to a meagre land holding is equivalent to poverty. Such poverty compels parents to view children as a substitute asset to land – it is believed that children can extricate families out of poverty. It is thus that unequal land distribution is a cause of large family size. In addition, as we have seen, it is also responsible for environmental stress; if land distribution were to be made more equal then households would be spaced out, thereby reducing environmental stress. Furthermore, the expected fertility decline would also reduce environmental degradation. Interestingly, this Georgist view does not recognize population growth as an underlying cause of environmental degradation. The fundamental reason for both population growth and environmental degradation is thought to be unequal land distribution.

Georgist reform

The principles behind a concrete Georgist policy to reduce population growth and also alleviate environmental stress is as follows. Since no human has made land (including all natural resources), no person has a better claim to land than any other. Therefore, land cannot belong to anyone in principle. Of course, the state is excluded as well. However, anyone who invests in improving land has a right to the value of improvements made. The reasoning is that if anyone makes something using his own inputs then that artefact belongs to him.

Given these guidelines, George suggested the following principle to solve the land distribution problem: everyone should have access to land provided that they pay the economic rent of their tract of land. He suggested the policy of land value tax which works thus. Consider a piece of land. Estimate its annual rental value, that is, the total return which acrrues to land minus the returns to labour and capital in using it. Set land value tax equal to this annual rental value. In this way, land value tax gets at economic rent of land which users have to pay to use the land. In common parlance it would be called ground rent. George also thought that by capturing economic rent and thereby providing revenue, the government should also be able to reduce other taxes, say income tax. George did not prescribe the forcible appropriation of land for the purpose of redistribution. His prescription of land value taxation was a fiscal device that would remove the institutional wedge between the land owner and the landless: using the revenue from land value taxation to reduce income tax would benefit the landless labourer; the tax would also discourage large land holdings, particularly for speculative purposes.

If taxes are a redistributive device, then isn't there the usual trade-off between equity and efficiency? The trade-off would certainly matter if there were increasing returns to scale – an empirical question, although the Georgists believe that most large holdings are inefficient. Another objection to land value taxation's redistributive role is the empirical observation that most peasants don't pay income taxes. There is also the real practical problem of bureaucracy and corruption when it comes to administering the tax. In addition, there is the problem of arriving at the correct tax rate. It is important to get the rate right first time since tax rates tend to be sticky. Finally, even though a land value tax is targeted on a minority, that minority is politically powerful and may be able to block its implementation.

Nevertheless, the nature of the point made by the Georgists is an important one: if you can get an economy to work more efficiently, then that is good for prosperity, the environment and also reduces overpopulation. By extension, one could then think of other impediments to efficiency and their removal: if an economy is badly managed then a managerial shake-up is called for; if the economy's investment record is poor then future investments have to be more carefully made; if the agricultural sector has been neglected then that has to be strengthened by diverting funds away from retail, industrial and service sectors; and so on – the list is a long one.

Suppose an indirect intervention, either a land value tax or some other sort, is successful. Would we eventually observe a fertility decline? Would the decline be a small one or a large one? We are back to the problems raised with the demographic transition theory itself (see Chapter 4). There we also voiced doubts about the effects of a prosperity induced fertility decline on the environment – after all there are close to three billion people in India, China and Africa and raising their prosperity by industrialization, say, could prove to be devastating to the environment. For these populations we need to consider other policy options just in case.

9.7 Conclusion

Three themes dominate this chapter: the mechanisms whereby prosperity induced fertility declines in industrialized economies; the problem of engineering prosperity in the first place; and the order in which countries become industrialized. The last theme connects with the next chapter.

While it is undeniably true that prosperity has been accompanied by a fall in fertility in Western Europe and the Far Eastern countries of Taiwan and South Korea, prosperity on its own is not enough – institutional changes are needed and the two such changes that seem to be important are urbanization (or the spatial arrangements whereby people live together) and nuclearization (or the make-up of the family unit). These changes raise the economic cost of child rearing and reduce the economic benefit of children.

Prosperity also needs to be accompanied by a third phenomenon: equality. An examination of the experience of Brazil and Mexico, where economic growth has been variable and benefited only a minority and where fertility decline has been patchy, suggests that broad-based growth might do the trick. Since wide inequalities in these countries can be traced to skewed land distributions, prosperity may be engineered by redistributing land. This, in fact, is the thesis of George and his followers who argue that redistribution by a land value tax would not only alleviate poverty and induce a fertility decline but also reduce environmental degradation. However, we have noted several problems with this sort of fiscal device for land redistribution.

Engineering prosperity for developing countries is not going to be easy. Perhaps the West and some of the Far Eastern countries have had it relatively easy being the first in the race to industrialize: we are clearly running out of both quantity and quality of the environmental capital which underpins economic growth. In any case, one could plausibly argue that the industrialized countries are overpopulated and overcrowded and this fate should be avoided for the developing countries. Therefore, as we turn to the major population growth problem of today – India, China and Africa – it appears sensible to think of more policy options.

10 Direct intervention

10.1 Introduction

The central proposition of the previous chapter was that prosperity eventually reduces fertility. This tenet was illustrated by the experience of Taiwan and South Korea. The route taken by these two countries is highly attractive since the outcome of greater prosperity and lower fertility is a kind of win–win situation. Interestingly, in both these countries governments played an active role in economic management and one can argue that at present countries which are having development problems and not experiencing significant fertility declines may have management problems.

One problem with the above mentioned win–win policy is that it ignores the question of optimum population size. Perhaps the question is irrelevant; Taiwan and South Korea may appear overcrowded but the people may be adequately compensated for overcrowding externalities by greater prosperity. However, even if one accepts this, one cannot help wondering whether the external costs of prosperous populations are, in fact, borne by less prosperous nations. If so, then for the sake of the welfare of the entire planet, the question of population size in already large populations such as Taiwan and South Korea needs to be reopened. In addition there is the problem of other countries which already have large populations and are keen to become prosperous.

Accordingly, this chapter begins by recounting the experience of India and China (sections 10.2 and 10.3). Both countries have large populations and have pursued neo-Malthusian population control policies which are different from those of Taiwan and South Korea. India has had very limited success with her attempts at centrally directed control of fertility whereas China has succeeded in reducing family sizes by what are perceived as coercive measures.

Both the South East Asian islands' experience and the Indian and Chinese experiences provide lessons in policy (sections 10.3–10.9). It is illuminating to apply these lessons to sub-Saharan Africa (sections 10.10–10.11). This region is particularly interesting because, although it appears to be under-populated, its population is growing rapidly. As such, sub-Saharan Africa presents an opportunity of meeting the optimum population size target without overshooting. Which policy will work: prosperity raising or neo-Malthusian or a neat combination of the two? Our conclusions are gathered in section 10.12.

10.2 The experience of India

In much of the Indian sub-continent, along a broad northern swathe encompassing Pakistan, the Indian states of Uttar Pradesh, Madhya Pradesh and Bihar, and

Bangladesh, fertility decline has been excruciatingly slow. (In some of the southern India states and Sri Lanka fertility has dropped significantly.) Overall, India's fertility has fallen from about 6 children per family to about 4 over four decades. UN projections, which assume rapid fertility decline to replacement level in South Asia, point to a 70 per cent population increase over the next 30 years in the region, in contrast to 28 per cent in East Asia. India is expected to overtake China in population size by about 2030.

South Asian social structure is a complicated picture of caste and class-riven village society. It appears that the central governments have to work hand-in-hand with local elites who often have their own objectives. However, changes are taking place at a slow pace: there has been a shift towards nuclearized autonomy and reduced parental expectations of old-age support from their children.

Unlike Brazil and Mexico, India has a large public sector and government intervention is attempted in many spheres of everyday life. Unlike China, the role of the Indian government in the development process has been ambiguous: meddling but undemanding in important respects.

A family planning programme was begun in India in the early 1950s and under Health Ministry auspices took on the heavily bureaucratized features of other Indian government initiatives. Programme targets and performance statistics had to be conveyed through a multi-layered hierarchy able to diffuse accountability and inclined to exaggerate results.

At first, at the heart of India's family planning programme was the idea of monetary incentives to reduce family size. It meant 'buying' fewer births with transistor radios and it did not work. The economic reason is that the planners miscalculated the 'terms of trade' at which babies and consumer goods are 'traded off'. But there may have been political and civil rights reasons as well. Although force and administrative pressure have been generally absent, apart from a short period during the emergency of 1975–6, it cannot be ruled out that there is still widespread resentment against India's now more comprehensive family planning programme. Moreover, large inter-state differences in programme effectiveness have emerged, reflecting distinctive administrative cultures and local socio-economic conditions. Incidentally, Pakistan and Bangladesh have similarly well-established family planning programmes with either negligible (Pakistan) or modest (Bangladesh) success records.

There are exceptions and the Indian state of Kerala is a good example (Sen, 1994). There, the birth rate has fallen sharply, on an annual basis, from 4.4 per cent in the 1950s to 2.0 per cent in the late 1980s. The reasons appear to be improved health and greater education. By improved health is meant greater life-expectancy and lower mortality rates and by greater education is meant widespread female education. The reasoning is not obvious and there is a suspicion that health and education correlate with more fundamental factors such as increased child rearing costs, reduced child benefits and greater economic security.

10.3   The experience of China

In terms of birth-rate decline, China more than matches Kerala's success. At the last count the birth rate was annually 2.1 per cent and moving towards 1.9 per cent. Moreover, this has been achieved in a surprisingly short period of time. On the other hand the unquantifiable costs may have been high because China relied on coercive direct intervention. These costs have to do with restriction on freedom and personal trauma.

The 1950s in China were characterized by massive agrarian reforms. Land reform and collectivization at a lower level were built on village solidarity and an absence of landlord and lineage interests. The village and the commune or township gradually took over some of the responsibilities normally placed upon the family. Local territorial solidarity was reinforced by agricultural taxes imposed on local units and by the pressure on the units to find many of their own social services. The boundaries of local units were further accentuated by government restraints on migration and economic diversification.

Complementing the above devolution was China's strong party structure which could apply central directives with their attendant rewards and penalties. This structure effectively delivered health services with life-expectancy reaching 65 years, so it is a little disconcerting to note that there was no effect on the rate of population growth. Therefore, in the 1970s, China embarked on direct measures to reduce family size. The state poured resources into family planning services accompanied by sanctions (for example, ration cards, basic social security and economic rights such as housing were made conditional on following the government's fertility objective), political pressure and exposure to public shame. The objective was to have two children per couple generally and one child per couple in the poorest areas. Fertility dramatically declined. Interestingly, the Dengist reforms after 1979 maintained the stringent controls over fertility and even attempted to extend one child per family target to all areas but this has proved to be exceedingly difficult to achieve.

One interpretation of the Chinese experience is that the government intervened to reduce fertility and thereby raise everyone's welfare since it perceived a prisoner's dilemma situation. In this scenario, every couple wants the maximum number of surviving children but the collective consequences of every couple acting in this way is fewer surviving children. Since people cannot break out of such a dilemma by unilateral action, intervention is justified. It is unlikely that the government could have intervened to the extent it did had there been great public resistance to smaller families. However, there have been two related unintended consequences of China's success in achieving fertility decline. First, as many Chinese think it is terrible not to have a son to carry on their name, there was a sharp rise in female infanticide. Baby daughters were killed in rural areas and pre-natal scans brought abortions of female foetuses in urban areas. Second, after 25 years of this, China has considerably more boys than girls in the sexually very active age group of 25 and younger. This has had some undesirable (?) consequences such as making prostitution a lucrative occupation.

10.4   Subsidies for childless women

If the goal of a given couple is to have the maximum number of surviving children that it can afford, then an increase in the cost of rearing children should reduce planned family size. Interestingly, the Chinese authorities did attempt to raise the cost of the marginal child by introducing severe penalties for extra child bearing. To raise the cost of child rearing in a more humane manner, one could think of providing a subsidy to women without children. Start with a young girl who does not have any children. Let such a girl be entitled to draw a regular subsidy as long as she stays childless. This unearned income is withdrawn once she bears a child. There is therefore an incentive for the woman to postpone child bearing. The principle behind the incentive is easy to understand: it is costly to have the marginal child. Of course, the strength of the incentive will depend on the size of the subsidy. This subsidy scheme can be refined by inversely relating subsidy to the number of children.

There may well be operational difficulties with the subsidy scheme. The scheme needs an army of bureaucrats and bureaucrats are susceptible to corruption. There is also the incentive to take advantage of imperfect information by drawing on the subsidy and also having children and hiding them. Worse, there is also the incentive to practise infanticide. Finally, there is the question of financing the subsidy.

10.5   Tradeable birth permits

Similar in principle to the subsidy scheme, that is, raising the cost of child rearing, is the tradeable birth permits plan (Boulding, 1964; Daly, 1974, Heer 1975). This plan delegates the scale and distribution of the right to bear children to some central authority (who can pay attention to the question of optimum population size) but requires that these rights be traded in a competitive market.

The tradeable birth permits idea is based on the premise that the right to reproduce should be a scarce good instead of a free good. However, presently the actual cost or price facing private couples is perceived to be 'too' low and the social cost 'too' high so that an increase in the private cost of reproduction needs to be engineered. The plan works as follows. Suppose the replacement number is two children per couple. Each couple then receives two permits, each permit giving the right to have one child. Once allocated, these permits can be bought or sold in a (hopefully) competitive market. Thus those who want more than two children would have to buy the appropriate number of permits whereas those who want one child or none could sell their allocation. Thus the scheme provides an economic incentive to have smaller families.

One feature of the plan is that it relates family size to wealth. In all probability, the extra child is then borne by a couple that can afford the responsibility of nurturing a new human being. As a consequence, the welfare of children is placed ahead of the right to reproduce freely. However, it also means that the wealthy can corner the market and raise the permit price beyond the reach of the non-wealthy. Another difficulty, and a very serious one, concerns penalty for those who have children without a permit. Is the child in question then simply a commodity to be passed on to a foster parent? Would the natural parents be tempted to kill the child if it is to be taken away from them? All sorts of possible trauma could manifest in such a situation.

10.6 Large young with human capital gamble

One alternative way of raising the cost of child rearing is to have each child endowed with more human capital, that is education plus health. The idea is to make parents bear the cost of human capital investment. Then, according to the micro-ecological model of large young with human capital gamble, fertility should decline since only, say, two educated and healthy children are as affordable as six without human capital. However, this policy has a flavour of compulsion and that means that there would be a reduction in parental happiness. So, first, we need to ask why parents do not go for a highly endowed small family. One such situation is that in which parents perceive that in a highly competitive world, two well-endowed children do have greater survival chances than six badly-endowed children but that either the human capital investment is not otherwise worthwhile or the investment is not accessible. It is not worthwhile when the rate of return to human capital is greater than the market lending rate but less than the market borrowing rate and parents have zero assets. It is not accessible when the rate of return to human capital is the highest of the three rates but the parents face credit rationing. That happens when they have no collateral and the lender cannot distinguish between honest and dishonest borrowers. Is there anything that a government can do about this?

10.7 Fertility, capital formation and supply side growth

In section 10.10 we shall list the conditions under which a government may be able to secure funds in order to subsidize health and education. In this section we look at another way in which a government may be able to intervene meaningfully in these areas. It is sometimes the case that groups of a country's population are discriminated against and thereby prevented from having access to health and education investments. In the context of fertility, women are the most telling example of a discriminated group. It is thought that social customs prevent girls from fulfilling their health and education potential and, furthermore, the social rate of return to a girl's education investment is higher than a boy's. The reason is that it is thought that increasing a girl's education translates into reduced fertility which in turn reduces consumption demand releasing resources for capital formation thereby raising output in a supply side model. Thus Thurow (1994) has forecast that India will not join the wealthy industrial world since it has not had at least a century in which her population grew at no more than 1 per cent. He thinks that it is impossible for a country to get rich if its population is growing at a fast rate because resources are committed to meeting the basic demands of children. To take another example, in 1990 a Kenya Demographic and Health Survey estimated the population of Kenya at 24.6 million, with an annual growth rate of 3.8 per cent. Using these figures, the 1996 population must have been about 30.8 million and the 1997 population 31.9 million. Kenya's population is therefore growing by more than a million a year with the highest increase being among the poorest people, who make the largest proportion of the population. To educate, say, a maximum of one million extra children annually would require an extra million places to be made ready every year from 1996. At 1 000 pupils per school, 1 000 new schools will be needed a year, or three new schools every day. All these demands are in addition to the huge unsatisfied current needs of Kenya. Evidence of declining quality of education in Africa and Latin America also confirms the view that education investment suffers when fertility rates are high (Birdsall and Sabot, 1993). For example, the absolute size of the school-age population in Mexico increased by 60 per cent from 1970 to 1989. Education expenditure also increased by 60 per cent, just enough to maintain per child spending on education. There is also evidence at the family level that high fertility inhibits investment in children's education. A study of families with twins in India found that the additional unexpected child represented by twins reduced enrolment levels of all children in the household (Rosenzweig and Wolpin, 1980). Estimates based on Malaysian data showed that couples with a higher biological propensity to have births are also characterized by lower schooling attainment for their children (Rosenzweig and Schultz, 1985). Clearly, lower fertility at family level can have a positive effect on education and eventually encourage economic growth.

Turning to an earlier assertion, why should an increase in female literacy reduce fertility? First, education increases the potential wages that women can command; in this way, it raises the value of women's time and so adds to the effective cost of child bearing. Second, better educated women tend to marry later. Third, education confers power. It is thought that within a household women have a weaker bargaining position than men, partly because of cultural and social norms. Once established, such norms are difficult to alter since it is thought that a whole community respects them and a woman who questions the norms is likely to face community sanctions (see Chapter 7). However, empowering women with education could trigger off a change in the norms. If that happens then the cost of child rearing would also have to be borne by the hitherto free-riding men who may then consent to having a smaller family (see Perusse, 1993). In addition to directly challenging social norms, education can weaken social norms by raising women's economic power. Job prospects for educated women and hence women's economic power should improve as electronics and other women's jobs gain in importance at the expense of brute-strength ones (including peasant farming). This should translate into more influence for a woman within a household over fertility decisions. Turning to evidence, studies from individual countries point out that one extra year of female schooling can reduce the fertility rate by between 5 per cent and 10 per cent. A simulation study of 72 countries around the world showed that, if all other factors were held constant, doubling female secondary-school enrolments in 1975 would have reduced the average fertility rate in 1985 from 5.3 to 3.9 children and lowered the number of births by almost 30 per cent (*The Economist*, 2 September 1995). Incidentally, as well as having fewer children, educated women are more likely to have better fed, and therefore healthier, children who will themselves be better educated. Evidence from World Bank Surveys in Nicaragua, Pakistan, Vietnam and Côte D'Ivoire suggests that the probability of a child being in school increases with the mother's own education.

Finally, the policy of educating women may have a large pay-off – women account for two-thirds of the world's illiterates, and three-fifths of the world's near 150 million denied access even to primary education are girls.

10.8   Contraceptives
It is thought that education also imparts information about contraceptives and that information helps reduce fertility. The belief – that there are a great many unwanted babies in the third world and that such pregnancies could have been avoided if people had known about contraceptives and also had access to them – is widespread. The theory behind the belief is that in the course of their everyday life, people make mistakes out of ignorance. There is very little evidence to support the above outlined belief – only sketchy survey evidence which asks married women retrospective questions (see Hill, 1992). These surveys are poorly designed and do not check if the elicited answers are true or what the respondents are expected to say.

According to the micro ecological model, a couple wants the maximum number of children it can afford and if the number is six, say, then the couple will opt for six children and use the tool of contraceptives to prevent any further pregnancies. Contraceptives are a convenient tool, in whose absence the couple might have used some other, more cumbersome, tool. Additionally, ecological thinking also predicts that contraceptives can eventually lead to a larger population. Here is the reasoning. Suppose a couple wants six healthy and educated children. Resources are scarce and occur evenly over time. So it is best to space the six children out. Contraceptives are an efficient tool for this policy of spacing. The outcome is six spaced children who have a greater survival probability then six unspaced children. Hence, in the long run, population size must increase. Earlier, in Chapter 7, we cited West African evidence where African women do precisely this. They want many children, they want them spaced out and contraceptives help them to this end. Contraceptives are also used by older women to protect their health after the family size decision has been executed. Viewed thus, contraceptives are simply a better technique for perfecting the ancient breeding strategy; they have little effect on either how many children a couple *wants* or on resources and these, ultimately, determine family size. It appears that the real challenge is to get people to want fewer children than they can afford and the technological fix of contraceptives is a poor tool with which to achieve that goal.

10.9   Human capital and prosperity: a virtuous circle

We argued in section 10.7 that an increase in female human capital reduces fertility which implies, for any given amount of such investment, more non-human capital accumulation per worker and this raises output per head. However, there is an additional reason to think that human capital is beneficial for growth which is that it is an independent input in production. In cross-country empirical studies of growth, measures of the educational attainment of populations have been consistent and important factors behind growth success. More important, education appears to matter over and above its effect as an additional input in production; at the country and firm level, it is also associated with higher total factor productivity, that is, with higher output for given inputs (Pack and Page, 1993).

We take it that female education can foster prosperity. In turn, according to demographic transition theory, prosperity reduces fertility after a sizeable time-lag and in the earlier chapters we discussed the possible mechanisms that operate to accomplish this. If so, then it appears that a virtuous circle may be established: 1) Begin by making human capital accessible to girls, 2) that reduces fertility and 3) since human capital is an independent input in production, increases output. 4) In the longer run, lowered fertility also raises non-human capital, another input in production. 5) Increased output, doubly boosted, lowers fertility with a lag. 6) Prosperity also eventually raises human capital (Birdsall and Griffin, 1988; Birdsall, 1988; World Bank, 1984) and completes the virtuous circle.

What can go wrong? One awkward possibility is that of certificate escalation. Suppose that wages are sticky, at least in the short run, and that it is technical knowledge that really determines the number of jobs. Then, by assumption, investment in human capital is not immediately productive so that the collective consequence of individual education decision making is not prosperity but education certificate escalation. In the long run, however, fertility at least should fall and, also in the long run, education should advance technical knowledge.

The other practical problem is that of finance for investment in human capital. Actually, since human capital needs to work with non-human capital in the production process, we might take it that there is a problem of finance for all sorts of investments. So let us turn to the problem of financial bottlenecks in the context of Africa's population growth problem.

10.10   Raising Africa's prosperity

Africa, as is well known, has a very high population growth rate. Yet Africa, unlike China or India, may not, as yet, have exceeded its optimum population size. To meet its optimum size without overshooting, Africa could emulate China's fertility decline success. However, as we noted, the Chinese experience was somewhat inhumane although in sections 10.4 and 10.5 two more humane alternatives were suggested, taxes on children (or subsidies for childless women) and tradeable birth permits respectively. The biggest problem in implementing either of these is political, such a policy being a vote-loser. In addition to this, there are the problems noted in the earlier sections.

So it looks as if one policy option Africa has of not exceeding its optimal population size will not be exercised. Nevertheless, can Africa achieve some reduction in its fertility rate by some other means? From the discussions of the previous sections one could appeal to raising health and education levels, particularly those of women. Africa also needs to invest in newer non-human capital. The problem as we noted in section 10.9, is one of finance.

Now it appears that the South East Asian economies (Taiwan, South Korea, Singapore, Malaysia and Thailand in particular) have been able to invest partly because of their high private saving rates. In addition to the high propensity to save, the governments of these countries also applied pressure to save. For instance, the Singaporean government forces every employee to save 20 per cent of his/her earnings and this is matched by an equivalent contribution by employers.

In addition to a low rate of saving, African countries are heavily indebted and need revenues to service the debts. It is interesting to note that the reason for indebtedness is poor quality investment. Many of the public funded projects in Africa have underperformed. Where the projects were financed by borrowed money, the revenues generated fell short of interest payments on debt. Africa is indebted because the continent has not created wealth from its borrowings.

An African government may be able to divert funds from an area such as defence expenditure to another area such as health and education expenditure. It depends on how the social rates of return to expenditure in these competing areas are perceived. A government such as that of Ethiopia (or Pakistan) may regard both areas as public goods but, facing external threat from Somalia (or India) may deem that the return on defence expenditure is higher. On the other hand we have had the examples of Taiwan, South Korea and Singapore where each government unambiguously gave a low priority to defence and a high priority to health and education. More recently, the president of Haiti abolished the 7000 man army, releasing 40 per cent of the national budget for possible investment in health and education.

Another source of finance is aid which in the past has been relatively generous to Africa. However, more recently, the donor nations have been either reducing aid or attaching stringent conditions to it. The donor countries have, of course, noted with concern the failure of past aid-backed projects and have attributed the failures to mismanagement and corruption (although it may be added that some bad advice was also given). Therefore, to receive further aid, and also to have debts partially written off, the African countries need to demonstrate competence. This may prove to be a difficult task. For example, it is thought that corruption is so deeply entrenched that one could say the whole public system – the civil servants, the police, the judiciary, the politicians and so on – is corrupt. Then the private incentive to practise corruption is very strong. As in a prisoner's dilemma, any individual who unilaterally stays honest is a sucker. Another impediment to competence is lack of unity due to tribal divisions, something that is absent in the South East Asian countries. Once again, this is a deeply entrenched problem, made worse by leaders whose *raison d'etre* is to perpetuate their own powers. Various means are deployed to hang on to power: buying loyalty from the army, co-opting the political class and ignoring the rule of law. Tribal enmity and its perpetuation also creates a culture of violence, quite unlike the culture of non-violence that prevails in the South East Asian economies.

There is a vicious circle in the making here. The population is largely uneducated. That enables the African leaders to perpetuate a culture of corruption and violence. That leads to economic mismanagement. That discourages aid for investment in health and education. Since education should be conducive to change, the situation remains the same or worsens.

A further problem with whatever aid given to Africa is the set of conditions attached to it. In particular, the donor nations specify the kind of development for which aid should be used. Most aid to African countries requires the recipients to participate more in international trade by playing to their comparative advantages. This, of course, implies specialization which carries great risk, especially given Africa's rising human population. Consider the scenario in which an African country exports a cash crop to pay for its imports which include food. Suppose that, perhaps due to favourable weather conditions all over the world, there is an increase in the supply of the cash crop causing its price to fall. Then the exporting African country may not be able to generate enough revenue to pay for its imports. With the resulting shortage of food, a Malthusian crisis scenario could easily materialize.

10.11   World inequality

A different yet illuminating perspective on the prosperity problems of many of the third world countries and, by implication, policy action on population growth, is obtained when we examine global inequality and its persistence. At issue is the possibility that any increase in world prosperity will show up as the rich nations becoming richer with the poor remaining poor. First, a few trends.

Before the expansion of Europe and industrialization there were little differences in wealth between the main agricultural societies. The first settled societies and early empires such as Babylon, Egypt, Syria, Persia, Macedonia, Rome, the Han in China and the numerous Indian states were all agricultural societies with roughly similar structures and dependent on much the same technology, and their relative wealth varied mainly according to the gains made from temporary success in war and the expropriation of the wealth of the defeated. Medieval China, India and Europe were also at roughly the same stage of development – still essentially agrarian with a tiny industrial sector and limited trade.

The distribution of wealth in the world became increasingly unequal in the period after 1500. Perhaps this was due to unequal control over the world's resources. Europe controlled many regions of the world and a considerable part of the wealth that was invested in commerce and industry in Europe after 1500 came from the newly founded colonies. It is also likely that the control exercised over the earth's resources by Europe, USA, Canada, Australasia and Japan underpinned the great industrial expansion of the nineteenth and twentieth centuries.

In any case, there has resulted a high unequal economic world. It appears that the industrialized countries do utilize the vast majority of the world's resources. To trot out a well-known statistic, the US supports roughly 5 per cent of the world's population but it uses 40 per cent of the world's mineral and 30 per cent of its energy resources. It is believed that the average American consumes the same amount of resources every year as 25 Indians. In contrast, nearly 60 per cent of the inhabitants of the third world (over 1 billion people) still lack basic human requirements such as adequate food, drinking water and shelter.

The world has been characterized by wealth inequality for five centuries. Will global inequality persist? The answer is yes if environmental constraints on technical progress bind. For then third world economic growth will prove to be difficult to achieve since there will be no 'spare' resources to enable third world countries to industrialize. It is also highly unlikely that the rich nations will be willing to lower their standard of living in order to aid the poor nations. The new challenge will then be in applying human ingenuity (technical progress, greater efficiency, better management, and so on) to raise everyone's material prosperity without incurring adverse environmental external effects.

10.12   Conclusion

This chapter can be looked at as a comparison of neo-Malthusian policies (subsidies for childless women, tradeable birth permits) with prosperity promoting policies (raising health and education levels, investing in infrastructure, improving management of the economy).

Neo-Malthusian policies are based on ecological thinking. It is believed that the collective and environmental consequences of people's inherent, uncontrollable tendency to procreate are extremely serious. Since voluntary control of fertility is weak, intervention is needed to strengthen control and arrive at the optimum population size. In the instance where the actual population exceeds the optimum, neo-Malthusians would not hesitate contemplating population size reduction to arrive at the optimum. Such thinking challenges the presumption that birth control is more desirable than abortion which is more desirable than infanticide which is more desirable than child mortality. For instance, some neo-Malthusians advocate euthanasia as a policy tool. In the instance where the actual population falls short of the optimum size but population growth is rapid, neo-Malthusians advocate prevention and the method favoured is an increase in the cost of child rearing. Finally, it is believed that the cause of poverty is population size so the idea is to first get the population size right and let prosperity follow.

As far as prosperity promoting policies are concerned, the idea is to prioritize prosperity and then let population size adjust. Since population growth is voluntarily expected to fall with prosperity, such a policy is regarded as a win–win policy. The policy is favoured by economists although when it comes to raising prosperity it has to be recognized that technical progress is a key factor, although not the only one, in driving it. As for any external effects of population size, it is believed that people can be compensated for the adverse externalities with greater prosperity. So population size does not really matter if enough prosperity can be generated. Clearly these are not preventive policies, more of a curative kind.

A neat combination of the above two stances is human capital powered growth. Such a policy raises costs of child rearing, immediately causing a fertility decline long before greater prosperity materializes. There are, however, three related major questions: 1) can human capital investment deliver prosperity on its own? 2) Will we not quickly run out of environmental capital if rapid economic growth takes root worldwide? 3) Will the rich nations share their technical knowledge and control of the environment – two factors which are complementary to human capital in order to generate growth – with the poor nations? If not, then come the next century will we find the majority of people living in urban squalor and the minority in urban affluence?

PART IV

WHEREIN LIES THE FUTURE?

11   An urban future

11.1   Introduction

Never before in the history of our species have so many people lived on such small spaces of land. Instead of being evenly spread across the earth, we have tended to cluster together in large urban environments. For example, three-quarters of the US population now live in an urban milieu with the result that approximately 70 per cent of the population occupy 3 per cent of the land.

We argued in the previous chapters that an important mechanism by which fertility declines is urbanization. Like the laboratory bottle in which flies live and multiply, the urban environment acts as a spatial constraint on fertility. However, as long as food resources are supplied, it takes a while before the 'urban brake' is applied so that there is a phase during which we observe an increase in both population and urbanization.

Not surprisingly, we are currently witnessing on-going population growth and expanding cities, at least in the third world, and hypothetically 24 additional cities of 3 million are created every year. In fact, we are at a turning point in human history: the point at which the balance of Earth's population decisively shifts from rural living to urban living. By the millennium, it is expected that half the world's humanity will live in large urban areas. In fact, whereas back in 1975 the proportion stood at one-third, by 2025 it is expected to rise to nearly two-thirds.

The net effect of our two urges – the tendency to procreate and the tendency to live in clusters – has been to place enormous pressure on living space. Thus over 130 cities in the world now have a population of over 1 million. Accordingly, the question posed in this chapter is this: does living closely packed together matter for our collective welfare?

The answer rests on the analytical distinction made between affluent cities and third world cities. Although affluent cities may suffer from adverse overcrowding externalities (sections 11.2 and 11.3) these may be compensated for by beneficial externalities (section 11.4) and by affluence itself. However, it is likely that the burden of supporting this affluence is borne by poor rural areas and poor third world cities. Accordingly, section 11.5 takes a closer look at living conditions in third world cities. The emerging picture of human suffering prompts a search for policy initiatives (section 11.6). Section 11.7 collects the conclusions to this chapter.

11.2   Living conditions in the first world city

Compared to the village life of our ancestors, cities are full of strangers. In the primeval tribe of around 100 members, everyone knew everyone else. In the city, there are millions of strangers. It is possible that many of the problems of city life derive from the stresses impacting on sensibilities formed by the hunter-gatherer lifestyle of 10 000 years ago. Road rage, claustrophobia and crime are cited as among the penalties of city life.

Packed in a small area, the spatial dimension of territories has been considerably reduced in a city. This loss may matter because one of the most basic ways in which animals reduce aggression (and generally co-exist) is to form well-defined territories. These are defended spaces. By keeping to separate patches, everyone has a share of the environment. Each territory provides its owners with a spatially limited form of dominance, making it possible for them to respect the territory of others.

Crowding and behaviour in public and private places
Territorial boundaries become blurred with crowding. Then relationships between people can become less harmonious, increasing chances of conflict. It is worth making a distinction between interactions in public and private places since public places dominate city life. When people are in public places the territory is not marked for anyone in particular. To achieve cohesion that is necessary in the complex world of city life we need conventions of behaviour when in public places. Accordingly, city dwellers need to co-operate in a subtle set of rules about spacing in public places. Conventions, of course, require the agreement of others. Points of conflict arise when tacit agreements break down or are misinterpreted.

City life greatly increases such chances of conflict (Krupat, 1985). With great crowding in public places, the implicit rules of personal space in public places can become overwhelmed. There is also a greater opportunity for an individual to gain some personal advantage by breaking the implicit rules since the sanction of social disapproval in the city matters less compared to village life sanction. Even if conventions are adhered to so that cohesion is maintained and thereby conflict is contained, it means that, in public places at least, city dwellers are obliged to follow strict patterns of behaviour. That means some loss of freedom and individuality.

Turning to private places, where territory boundaries are expected to be observed, there is nevertheless a problem. Residents are packed together in a city and, as a result, there is residential crowding. That makes it much more difficult to find privacy or to avoid involuntary social contact.

City crime and violence
Large cities generally have higher levels of crime. (Criminal statistics are notoriously subject to error because many crimes are not reported to the police. This means that most figures underestimate crime.) Within countries, there seems

to be a direct relationship between the size of a city and the likelihood of crimes such as drug-taking, burglary and bodily attacks (Lynch, 1960).

Fear of violence and crime is a social problem because it limits the amount of voluntary social interaction that occurs. People who are most fearful of crime and violence in public areas are less likely to venture out and meet others. So fear alters behaviour – people avoid going to certain places at certain times and also avoid going out alone. In addition, restrictions on children's activities are thought to have increased because the fear of violence to children has grown (an interesting point is that the large majority of parents who restrict their children were not restricted themselves when they were children). Moreover, there are direct emotional effects of the fear – tension, anxiety – on parents and children (Apter, 1992).

Territorial spacing is one way in which levels of aggression can be relaxed. Another system is that of 'peck order' or social hierarchy and the theory is as follows (Morris, 1994). In the ancient smaller and simpler tribe, the distance between the top and the bottom of the peck order was not dramatic. However, the contrast between the status of the city's cardboard-box dwellers and the billionaire tycoons is vast. There are so many at the bottom and so few at the top that there are always some who will be driven to seeking revenge for what they see as their suppression and exploitation. Those squashed at the bottom and too cowardly to attack the powerful source of their agony turn to weaker victims – women, children and animals – who serve as substitutes. This may explain the prevalence of 'redirected aggression' or violence for the sake of violence in cities.

Stress
The pace of the lives of our ancestors was once ruled by the rhythm of the sun and the changing seasons. However, for today's city dwellers, speed has become part of their culture. We are working much harder than before and taking less leisure. In a city, a great deal has to be done and complex negotiations conducted in often difficult and rushed circumstances. So compared to their ancestors, city dwellers lead vastly accelerated lives. The increased speed required to do things, time urgency, can be distinguished from time pressure, the need to find more time to fit in all we have to do. It is time pressure that is thought to cause stress (Norman, 1988).

11.3 Adapting to city life
Overall stress is likely to be reduced when conventions of behaviour work in the city. However, what is special about stress in the city is that much of it is difficult to change: the city environment, which ultimately is responsible for stress (Halpern, 1995) has to change and engineering a re-plan of an existing city is extremely problematic.

In our distant past, we often altered the environment to suit us. Nowadays, it appears that we largely adjust to accommodate the demands of city life such as the noise, the crowds and the information overload. The kind of adaptation that has taken place goes something like this example: we become habituated to noise. When we experience a constant level of background noise, as we do in most cities, we tend to habituate to it such that we hardly notice it at all. Another example: we have responded to time pressure by doing things quickly and by adopting a mode of behaviour which makes the time we do have at our disposal more intense (for example, aerobics instead of long walks, talking on a mobile phone while driving). City life is also made up of a huge number of encounters with potential sensory and information overload. We adapt to this by tunnelling our attention – for example, when walking in a crowded street we do not stop and talk but keep our faces blank and eyes straight ahead. So city dwellers have adapted to a high level of noise, doing a great many things in a short time interval, crowds, information overload, and so on (Newman and Lonsdale, 1996).

Adaptation is costly and therefore welfare reducing. Adaptation also implies restriction of freedom or additional restriction on behaviour and therefore reduces welfare yet again. The problem is that we adapt behaviour to suit city environment. The solution is to re-plan cities to suit us.

One aside on adaptation: some hold the view that evolution by adaptation is the sole purpose of human existence. Then re-planning cities is only of value if the benefit of an enhancement of our survival chances (for instance, minimizing the risk of epidemics, see section 11.5) outweighs the cost of re-planning.

11.4   Beneficial externalities of city life

Despite the disadvantages of living in conditions so unnatural for our ancestors, the fact remains that, notwithstanding a trickle of people moving out of cities, millions of people do stay on in the cities of the affluent nations. One reason for this is straightforward: cities make a major contribution, primarily through industrial output and professional services, to the national economy and that provides employment.

In addition to employment, urban life must have some powerful appeal to, at least, a sizeable minority. The slow pace, peace and tranquillity of the countryside represents boredom and lassitude, monotony, conformity, lack of choice and the fear of being out of touch to some people. On the other hand, a large city in which there are a great many people in a relatively small geographical area contains diversity. That, in turn, can offer diverse opportunities for material advancement, artistic expression, consumption and lifestyle (Morris, 1994).

Most cities are also characterized by tolerance and acceptance of differences, and freedom from the constraints of tradition. The tolerance, freedom and diversity of the city creates a crucible for change. New ideas and attitudes evolve, old conformities and values are challenged and replaced. The city is responsive to innovations and to trying out new things that have not been done before. The city can be dynamic and that stimulates many people. It is not surprising to find that invention, science and the arts can flourish in the city: it is probably at the cutting edge of civilization. Finally, for the affluent at least, the city must offer greater choice although this must be balanced against the greater volume of rules and regulations on social behaviour that are necessary to oil the wheels of any city if it is to function properly.

From a welfare perspective, city life in the affluent West is somewhat of a paradox. Consider examples of southern immigrants into northern cities. Initially, the immigrants are cold, miserable and yearn for their warmer homelands. Over the years, however, most settle down, come to terms with a highly artificial and technology-driven environment, and are reluctant to return. It seems that adaptation changes preferences. Normally, one would have thought that having to adjust implies a loss in welfare. But it doesn't appear to be the case as far as city life is concerned. Does it imply that we can adapt to virtually any environment so that conventional notions of welfare and happiness have no meaning? That survival and adaptation is the sole aim of our existence? But even if we take the stance that successful adaptation to a changing environment is the sole motive of our existence, large cities may not be at their optimum sizes. This is because city life does have external effects on people not living in cities; some communities elsewhere have to bear the costs of supporting our affluent cities. These societies are found in rural areas of the world and also in third world cities.

11.5   Third world cities

Whereas there is a slow drift to rural areas from the cities in the affluent countries, there is a large scale migration to third world cities from third world rural areas. In fact, the twentieth century has witnessed the urbanization of the third world at a far faster rate than that of the developed world's in the nineteenth century. Then the fastest rate of growth in the urban population was 2.5 per cent a year but in the twentieth century the third world's equivalent annual growth rates were 3 per cent before 1940 and 4 per cent thereafter (the latter figure is enough to double the urban population every 18 years). In fact, in some countries, major cities have increased in size at even faster rates. Overall, the most rapidly urbanized area in the world has been Latin America with growth rates of over 5 per cent a year in the 1950s. By the 1980s, about two-thirds of the people of Latin America were living in cities. Currently, Asia and Africa remain mainly rural – about a third of the population live in cities. But urban populations are large because of large country populations.

The rapid urban growth rates have had the following serious impacts. The infrastructure of a third world city is under immense strain. Unemployment is high: in many cities 20 per cent of the people are unemployed and in some cities the percentage is even higher. Cities also reflect the great social inequalities found

ly in developing countries, particularly in Latin America. Housing is an
ous problem. At least a third of the population in the third world cities
live in illegal squatter settlements, usually on land designated as unsuitable for
housing by the authorities. Waste disposal – with the attendant health hazards
– is a growing problem in the third world. But perhaps the most serious
consequence of overcrowding and hence population size is the following.

Spread of viruses

There are precedents for the scenario in which as a result of high population
density, lowered defence mechanism and the abundance of unclean water, a new
disease spreads rapidly. Thus when European rabbits contracted myxomatosis,
98 per cent of them died within six months. The same scale of mortality is entirely
possible in humans, should a similar virus infect tightly packed urban areas. The
city habitat, with its high population of constantly moving and mingling people,
all living in warm surroundings and within close proximity of uncollected
waste and dirty water, is a good breeding and transmission medium for diseases.
The mechanism is as follows. Any species that overcrowds itself beyond a certain
point shows the following stages of damage. 1) Individuals become
psychologically stressed causing physiological disturbances. (If lemmings
overbreed in a particular season, they soon start to suffer from stress diseases
and rush madly in all directions.) 2) As a result, the body's immune system is
weakened making individuals increasingly vulnerable to infection. (Lemmings
exhaust their body defence mechanisms until, finally, most of them die from
stress-related diseases.) 3) The overcrowding makes it possible for infections
to spread like wildfire, turning into epidemics which decimate the populations.

Already flu epidemics have killed more people than the whole of human
warfare. Even if we succeed in building up some immunity, there is a twist.
Disease-creating bugs are constantly mutating, and because their life cycles are
so short, their evolution is rapid. The common cold is an excellent example. Just
as we build up an immunity to one form, it mutates into something slightly
different that cannot easily be dispatched by our antibodies. It is possible that
a more virulent, lethal disease can mutate and become as easy to catch as the
common cold. One method of protection is to ensure that our natural defence
mechanisms are not in a weakened condition. This means reducing urban stress
as much as possible. Another method is to reduce population density. This means
spatially spreading people out.

11.6 Unplanned growth

It appears highly likely that more and more people will live in urban areas. Not
only are more cities likely to emerge, existing third world cities are on an
expansionary course. One method for mitigating the expected adverse external

effects is to plan our cities. In this context, it is instructive to see the role of planning in the history of cities.

Before 1800 most cities in the world were small. Then, in the nineteenth century, cities began to sprawl, incorporating fields and villages. Most city growth was unplanned, the result of speculative development, often following the building of new transport systems as commuting became widespread (Sjoberg, 1960, Sutcliffe, 1984). The character of the suburbs was also dependent on the price of land. In the US, where land was generally cheap, the density of settlement was far lower than in Europe and so US cities spread over far larger areas (Chudacoff,1975). In Europe, concentrated industrialization in the nineteenth century also brought about the formation of the first conurbations – large formless urban masses caused by the expansion and joining up of a number of smaller settlements without a single urban focus (Hohenberg and Lees, 1985).

During the twentieth century, cities continued to grow in an unplanned manner, with transport again acting as one of the key determinants. The most significant development was the rise of the private motor car. The facility to drive independently to work affected settlement patterns in the US as early as the 1920s. Increasing car ownership strengthened the tendency of cities to sprawl over even bigger areas and for commuting distance to work to rise still further (Flink, 1975).

The growth of the cities was unplanned with the authorities trying, but failing, to influence development and to control numbers. The relatively weak planning controls in the UK, for example, have only managed to avoid some of the worst excesses of urbanization and in the US controls have been even weaker and less effective. The planned Soviet economy also failed to control the urban problems of Moscow. In 1935 a limit of five million inhabitants was put on Moscow. However, even with Stalin's authority and the introduction of an internal passport system, the limit was easily breached. In 1971 another limit of seven and a half million (the then current level) was imposed with a planned contraction to six and a half million by 2000. The current population is just over 10 million and there are the omnipresent lengthy commuting times, sprawling satellite towns and poor quality living conditions.

11.7   Policy

It is clear that the kind of environment in which we live has a massive impact on our behaviour. If our cities are like old-fashioned zoos, then we will miserably pace up and down our zoo cages. Instead of living failure, we need to extract living success from our cities. In other words, instead of putting up with poor living conditions and suffering adverse external effects, can we thrive in urban stimulation? Will cities turn out to be breeding grounds for lethal diseases and epidemics or for human inventiveness and creativity?

The problem appears to be that cities have grown haphazardly to accommodate the masses with the result that the people have had to adapt to the city structure. Living conditions should improve if cities were to adapt to our needs. In other words, to contribute to our living success, cities need to be re-designed. A re-planned city should be stimulating, encouraging our creative, as opposed to destructive instincts. Architecture is a good example; bad architecture is depressing, good architecture is inspiring (Whyte, 1988).

Is city planning feasible? Referring back to the previous section on the history of city growth, it was noted that even the former Soviet Union was unable either to control the size of Moscow or plan its development. More recently, a team of architects was commissioned to design a new district of the fast-expanding Shanghai. Scarcely was the ink dry on the low-energy, low-pollution vision of a circular city where cars were left outside and public transport did all the necessary work within, before the enormous development of Shanghai overtook the city administrators. New Shanghai developed piecemeal, just as cities nearly always do.

It is difficult to avoid the feeling of powerlessness since central re-designing of cities appears near impossible. On the other hand, history has an idea for a solution to the problem. From the widespread social concern of the mid to late nineteenth century sprang the charitable housing movement, in the absence of anything solid being offered by the central government. It operated locally rather than regionally or nationally. Perhaps an accumulation of local initiatives offers the best hope for the new urban world.

11.8 Conclusion

The United Nation's Population Fund (UNFPA), 1995 predicts that there will be a continuing shift of rural populations to urban areas with 56 per cent of the global population expected to live in urban areas by 2015. This means that the urban population is expected to increase from 2.6 billion to 4 billion in just 20 years. The most rapid urbanization is expected to be in developing countries.

According to some of the previous chapters of this monograph, urbanization is an important mechanism whereby fertility declines. Perhaps it works as an environmental limit to habitation by reducing the spatial dimension to our 'territories'. In any case, the prediction is that both population and urbanization should eventually stabilize. But when that happens, it is likely to be a highly overcrowded urban world and human welfare may be adversely affected.

It is useful to make a distinction between first world cities and third world cities. Both suffer from external effects of population size. However, it is thought that first world cities also experience beneficial externalities such as stimulus, diversity, freedom of expression, choice and so on. In addition, first world cities are relatively more affluent and it is hypothesized that this compensates for the adverse external effects of crime, violence, stress, rules, regulations and so on. Even so, it is likely that the functioning of first world cities imposes external effects elsewhere – rural areas and third world cities, for instance.

Turning to third world cities, the reciprocal external effects there are of a more serious kind – a greater likelihood of spread of viruses, for example. In addition, since these cities are poor, there is little compensation for the adverse external effects.

The problem for territorial animals like us living in cities is the lack of the spatial dimension to our territories. It is as if we have been haphazardly packed together – hence the adverse external effects. One obvious solution, which could also preserve the beneficial externalities of city life, would be to pack ourselves better. That implies re-planning most of our existing cities.

Can the requisite re-planning be accomplished? Our record of centrally initiated re-planning is very poor. In addition, existing cities are growing haphazardly. On the other hand, private initiatives can spring up to take charge of re-planning.

12 Conclusions

12.1 The problem

The scale and the speed of world population growth with its impact on the environment is an important phenomenon. 10000 years ago there were 4 million of us. The 1996 estimate of world population is 5.8 billion. Forecasts are subject to enormous error: optimists believe that world population will stabilize at 12 billion whereas pessimists believe that it will continue to grow beyond that number unless either there is a major catastrophe or there is successful policy intervention. In any case, it is a phenomenon that appears worth explaining.

Momentarily leaving aside an attempt at explanation, should we regard the growth and the size of our population as a problem? The answer depends on the social impact of private procreation decisions. However, there is disagreement on the impact. Take population growth. Pessimists (neo-Malthusians) believe that we are entering an era of ecological uncertainty and if with continued population growth the worst outcome is realized then we could become extinct alongside many other animal species. Even less than the worst outcome implies major upheavals in our lives. In addition, the environment is likely to degrade further. Optimists think that human ingenuity will be able to foresee any adverse ecological impact and deal with it adequately. As for population size, the neo-Malthusians think that there is a quantity–quality trade-off: a smaller population is a happier population. This is because it is believed that the current population size has several adverse external effects which reduce human welfare. Thus we could enjoy a higher standard of living with a smaller population which reproduces forever than with a larger population which experiences a lower standard of living and may become extinct in finite time. Others disagree. They believe that there is no quantity–quality trade-off and an increase in population size means greater human happiness. The reasoning is that more people means greater human ingenuity. Human ingenuity also implies prosperity which more than compensates for any adverse external effects.

Policy implications depend on which view one takes. If having more people is judged to be beneficial then the implication is to encourage procreation. If one thinks that there might be adverse ecological implications but is also an optimist as well as a risk-lover then policy implications are minimal. If one is a pessimist and also highly risk-averse then there are drastic policy implications. Personal preferences of the policy maker aside, good policy is derived from an explanation of population growth and size and it is a summary of that which now follows.

12.2 The logic

[1] *Micro-decision making: the large young gamble*

To begin at the beginning, the dominant influence on our behaviour then was exerted by our genes. Accordingly, the hunting-gathering couple went for the maximum number of surviving children. Given a resource constraint and a great deal of uncertainty concerning survival of children, the couple practised the large young gambit.

[2] *Decision making: an increase in resources*

Our ancestors were also highly intelligent and succeeded in making simple tools and other artefacts with the implication that their access to resources increased. Accordingly, given their breeding goal, they were able to increase family sizes.

[3] *Decision making: influence of rationality*

Another distinguishing characteristic of our ancestors was group territoriality. There were two interesting consequences. One, communities sprang up which laid claims to areas of land that provided food and shelter. Second, communal living meant that behaviour was influenced by social customs and culture. Communities that got their social norms right had a greater survival chance than communities whose norms were out of step with the environment.

[4] *Population consequences*

As a result of [2] and [3] human population increased and also spread out such that by 8000 BC about four million of us were scattered all over the globe.

[5] *Eltonian Pyramid*

Nevertheless, the Earth was thinly populated with humans. The explanation is that our population size was constrained by resource availability and these were relatively scarce given that we were at the top of the Eltonian Pyramid (or 'the food chain').

[6] *The ability to change niche*

According to ecological thinking, an increase in resources precedes population growth. Thus our discovery of agriculture led to an unprecedented increase in resources which was quickly followed by a steady expansion of the world's human population. Ecologists view the discovery of agriculture as a momentous event in our history since it gave us the ability to change our niche at will in the grand scheme of things.

[7] *Institutions*

In addition to technical ingenuity, we developed institutions such as the market to expand resources even further. Markets facilitated a more efficient allocation of resources and they also permitted specialization.

Initially markets did not have to cope with any external effects of population size since we were thin on the ground.

[8] *Urban shift*
With the steady expansion of population, however, we also began living in city-states. One feature of this habitat was a loss of space and some of the city-states inevitably began to show symptoms of overcrowding.

[9] *The Dismal Theorem*
As population continued to grow, observers began to think about the collective consequences of people's tendency to breed. In due course, Malthus arrived at the conclusion that if couples did not change their breeding behaviour so that food output growth fell behind population growth and 'if the only check on population growth is starvation then population will grow until it starves' (Boulding, 1977).

[10] *The Utterly Dismal Theorem*
The ongoing phenomenon that has falsified Malthus's prediction so far has been the astonishing technical progress (in agriculture and elsewhere). However, if technical progress were to run out of steam, then 'if the only check on population growth is starvation, then any technological improvement will have the ultimate effect of increasing starvation as it allows a larger population to live in precisely the same conditions of misery' (Boulding, 1977).

[11] *The demographic transition*
Meanwhile, with the aid of technical progress and the colonization of Americas, Australasia and Africa, Western Europe became prosperous and, following a lengthy period of rapid population growth, the average family size became smaller. This phenomenon of an eventual fertility decline accompanying prosperity is called the demographic transition. This phenomenon requires an exogenous change (that is, technical progress, colonization) to get prosperity started.

[12] *Micro-decision making: the large young with human capital gamble*
The demographic transition can be explained by the ecological model of [1] extended to incorporate human capital. Equipping children with human capital (and the increase in the value of wife's time) raised the costs of child rearing, reducing the number of children a family could afford. In addition, the economic benefits of having children also fell.

[13] *Taste change yields another micro model*
The ecological micro model assumes that couples opted for the maximum number of children they could afford. Suppose, instead, that some couples viewed children as pure consumption goods and did not go for the maximum number of children they could afford. Then we would say that prosperity change was also accompanied by a taste change so that the ecological explanation is no longer the only one.

[14] *A substitute for hereditary immortality*
There were also technical changes which enabled us to produce works of art and science with potential for immortality. Such artefacts serve as a substitute for hereditary immortality and remove the need to opt for the maximum number of children one can afford. If many parents can afford an extra child but choose to spend money on themselves and on furthering their interests, then, once again, the ecological explanation is limited to a smaller set of breeding couples.

[15] *The large young with survival uncertainty gamble*
The micro model alluded to in [13] is based on certainty. However, survival uncertainty is a prime consideration for many third world families. If so, then such couples may still opt for the maximum number of children they can support at subsistence level but having exercised all their fertility options, they allocate resources for investment in only the most promising child. This non-egalitarian strategy imparts a large family bias.

[16] *Micro explanations and population heterogeneity*
We thus have three micro explanations for family size: [12], [13]–[14], and [15]. If we are willing to accept that people have differing tastes and face differing degrees of economic security then these diverse explanations are consistent. Thus [12] appears applicable to South East Asian economics, [13]–[14] to the affluent Anglo-Saxon West, and [15] to the sub-Saharan Africa.

[17] *Incomplete micro models*
All the micro models are based on a questionable assumption – the collective consequences of fertility decisions do not figure in private decision making. Thus, in the micro model of [15], the collectively induced misery of living in narrow niche-spaces does not influence the micro objective of having the maximum number of children. Likewise, in [13]–[14] it is perhaps incorrectly assumed that people are not averse to overcrowding.

[18] *Completing a micro model*
One way in which a micro model may be completed is by incorporation of external effects, for example, (dislike of) overcrowding, into the micro utility function. Then the analysis of the altered model should show a reduction in individual welfare. Note that besides overcrowding, there are other adverse external effects.

[19] *A variety of adverse externalities*
Some serious adverse collective consequences have been attributed to population growth, ranging from dislike of overcrowding to the spread of infectious diseases. More recently, concern has been raised about possible global catastrophes. One new occurrence is that of planetary inter-

connections which has two implications. One is that a small population growth in one part of the globe may have an adverse environmental impact on another (remote) part. The other is that the overall resilience of the planet's eco-system is lowered, thereby constraining technological progress and material prosperity.

[20]   *An identification problem*

Some observers think that the observed environmental external effects are not due to population size but other factors. For example, pollution in Eastern Europe may be due to economic mismanagement and incorrectly priced energy sources. However, good evidence now exists on the correlation between deforestation, loss of wildlife habitat and even global warming on the one hand and population size on the other. Nevertheless, *ceteris paribus*, links between various externalities and population size will always be difficult to establish.

[21]   *A unique human ability*

Assuming that there are, in fact, adverse external effects of population size we draw an insightful distinction between humans and other animal species. An ant, for instance, is born into a complex chemical environment where every small instruction has been laid down in advance. In contrast, we humans recognize the value of a larger world beyond our own narrow self-interest.

[22]   *A prisoner's dilemma problem*

Accordingly, many observers are able to view the human population problem as a prisoner's dilemma problem. Since the prisoner's dilemma is a non-zero sum game, there is the possibility of raising welfare of everyone concerned. However, since individual incentives to raising social welfare are lacking, some form of collective action is required.

[23]   *Welfare from an ecological perspective*

To judge changes in social welfare, we need a welfare criterion. From an ecological perspective, there is a well-defined objective: maximize the number of surviving children. Then, the population problem is a scale problem if, with an increase in population size, (local or global) resource support begins to collapse. It is also a prisoner's dilemma situation where each couple has the private incentive to have the maximum number of surviving children yet the collective outcome is that of decreased survival chances.

[24]   *Welfare from an economic perspective*

Economists have a well-defined objective as well: reduction in human suffering. Once again, there is a scale problem if population size and human suffering are positively correlated. One powerful way in which this relationship occurs is when there are adverse external effects of population size. Then there is a trade-off between population size and external effects such that everyone's private welfare loss of a smaller family size may be compensated for by a reduction in the adverse external effects.

[25] *A technological solution*

Most economists, however, also believe that technological progress can neutralize any adverse external effects. Moreover, technical progress is the engine of prosperity. However, one problem with a technological 'fix' is that it may take a long, long time. In the meantime, there may be irreversible damage to the environment. The other problem with the technological cure is that its benefits apparently do not trickle down to the poorer nations yet its costs do, pollution for example.

[26] *Limitations of a technological solution*

Even if technology has the potential to clean up the adverse external effects that impinge on us in the affluent world, we may still be exceeding the optimum population size if people dislike crowding. Affluent people usually have choice and we do observe them moving away from crowded inner cities to less crowded suburbia and the very affluent moving from suburbia to rural retreats.

[27] *Two questions to guide possible policy*

Nevertheless, it would be extremely difficult to work out the optimum population for any given country since there is usually not enough information. However, we could usefully ask, and explore answers to, two questions: first, how can the population growth of an affluent country experiencing slow population growth be reduced in order eventually to reduce its population size? Secondly, how can population growth of a poor country experiencing rapid population growth be reduced so as to stabilize its population at a smaller size than would otherwise be the case?

[28] *Do nothing*

Given our poor record of intervention, indeed some believe that at times intervention makes matters worse, a school of thought has emerged which believes that in the long run 'nature knows best'. Unfortunately, it appears that the population external effects are not only persistent, but also worsening. Indeed, it is feared that the resilience of the natural environment may finally snap, blocking our ability to innovate. We may also embark on an era of greater uncertainty and instability which would diminish most people's happiness.

[29] *Self-regulation*

Perhaps, if left to themselves, people will self-regulate family size. After all, people must realize that the social cost of procreation outweighs private benefits. However, people may be powerless to self-regulate. This is because conditions such as that of existence of small, stable communities may be absent. In addition, great heterogeneity amongst people – differing information, expectations, subjective discount rates, and wealth – makes reaching workable voluntary agreements difficult.

[30]   *Indirect intervention: land redistribution*

Would indirect intervention work instead? According to demographic transition theory, any intervention that removes inefficiencies in the economic system and thereby promotes prosperity can reduce fertility. One such intervention is land redistribution in the third world countries. It is argued that by eliminating monopolistic elements in land ownership, there results greater economic efficiency which is conducive to prosperity and also beneficial to the environment. Eventually, a fertility decline should ensue.

[31]   *Indirect intervention: investment in capital stocks*

Another way of engineering prosperity is to sacrifice consumption and use the savings to invest in factors of production, particularly human and non-human capital. This strategy is best illustrated by the experiences of Taiwan and South Korea where the governments took active steps in promoting such investment.

[32]   *Favourable conditions for South East Asia*

In connection with the experience of the South East Asian economies, it is important to bear in mind the role played by the natural environment and technology. The countries in question were able to import cheap raw materials and energy, dispose of waste freely and adapt western technological advances.

[33]   *Reasons for additional policy*

One could say that while the economies of South East Asia – South Korea, Taiwan, Indonesia, Thailand, Malaysia, Singapore, Hong Kong and so on – are becoming prosperous and have experienced a fertility decline, they could also be said to be overcrowded. If so, has greater prosperity adequately compensated for the overcrowding externalities? More generally, does the population of a South East Asian economy exceed its optimum size? Furthermore, has the acquisition of prosperity inflicted adverse externalities on the environment of the rest of the world? Has prosperity been achieved at the expense of the poor countries of the world?

[34]   *One more reason*

[33] prompts the thought that we ought to entertain the idea that additional policy is needed to reduce population size to its optimum. In other words, while the engineering of prosperity may succeed in reducing fertility, it may do so too slowly and with a sizeable lag.

[35]   *And another reason*

The final reason for additional intervention arises from the existence of countries that are poor, have large populations, and where population growth is high, for example, India. It could easily be the case that such countries do not have surplus resources for additional investment; in fact they may be fast running down their stock of environmental capital in order to meet the consumption demands of a large population and the basic investment demands of the growing young cohorts.

[36] *Direct intervention*

The Chinese experience suggests the policy option of direct intervention. The Chinese authorities presumed that most Chinese couples had the maximum number of children they could afford, regardless of the social consequences. Perceiving social benefits of smaller family sizes, the Chinese authorities imposed family size quotas accompanied by a range of fiscal penalties as well as direct coercion. This somewhat inhumane policy did succeed in reducing family sizes.

[37] *Humane direct intervention*

A more humane form of direct intervention is that of tradeable birth permits. In this scheme, the government sets the number of children each couple can have but subsequent to this, couples can buy and sell permits in a competitive birth permits market. Another policy device is to give incentive to childless women to stay childless by subsidizing their childless status. This is equivalent to taxing women with children. Most of the problems with these neo-Malthusian policies are of a practical kind.

[38] *Another human policy*

Humane neo-Malthusian policies work by raising child-rearing costs. One more way of raising such costs is to have each child endowed with more human capital. In fact, parents themselves may wish to invest in their children's education and health but are unable to do so. Social customs, for instance may discourage investment in girls.

[39] *Reason to favour investment in girls*

In fact, it is thought that the social rate of return to a girl's education investment is higher than a boy's. The reason is that it is thought that increasing a girl's education translates into reduced fertility which in turn reduces consumption demand releasing resources for capital formation and thereby raising output in a supply-side model.

[40] *A virtuous circle*

Furthermore, an increase in the level of women's human capital should directly raise a country's prosperity, human capital being an input in production of output. As a result, a virtuous circle may be established whereby investment in women's human capital immediately lowers fertility and in the long run raises prosperity both of which, in turn, boost further investment.

[41] *Opportunity to embark on virtuous circles*

For an application of [40] turn to third world countries that are experiencing high population growth rates, such as sub-Saharan African countries, and where it is theoretically possible to stabilize population levels at the optimum sizes without overshooting.

[42]   *Impediments to a virtuous circle*

The trick is to embark on the virtuous circle [40] which requires investment funds. There are serious doubts whether these counties can generate the requisite funds internally. Even if the countries can secure external aid, there are equally serious doubts whether the funds will be used for the intended purpose.

[43]   *Another impediment*

One further problem is the presence of environmental constraints. Most observers now accept that the challenge facing poor nations is to develop without further damaging the environment. A way out might be to persuade affluent societies to cut down on their consumption so as to release environmental resources for third world development.

[44]   *Affluence in first world cities*

Such a sacrifice is unlikely – the world has been characterized by persistent wealth inequality for five centuries. Interestingly, most of the consumption of the affluent societies is connected with living in sophisticated cities. It is thought that the affluence is required to compensate people for the overcrowding externalities associated with densely packed populations in modern western cities.

[45]   *Welfare in cities*

In addition to affluence, there are beneficial external effects of city life, especially a stimulating, liberal environment that is at the cutting edge of civilization. However, it is debatable whether these beneficial externalities, and affluence of course, outweigh the negative externalities of crime, fear, violence, stress, anxiety, living in a highly artificial environment and so on.

[46]   *Revealed preference*

Therefore, it is interesting to note that there is an on-going drift of people out of the larger first world cities despite the glue of state dependence (the phenomenon illustrated by Londoners who cannot contemplate living anywhere else). It is, in fact, the more affluent who are moving to the fringes of the city, away from the poverty and squalor of the inner cities where adverse externalities are likely to dominate.

[47]   *Third world cities*

Many of the third world cities are simply mega versions of the first world inner cities. Such places are melting pots of squalor, violence, crime and disease. Better planning of cities would help but history suggests that planners are rarely able to impose their planning ideas since growing cities have momentums of their own.

[48]   *A difference between ecologists and economists*
Alternatively, we could space ourselves out and not flock to cities. This illustrates an essential difference between ecologists (neo-Malthusians) and economists. While both accept that human beings are territorial, ecologists emphasize the importance of the spatial dimension to territories. Economists, on the other hand, think that prosperity (and the beneficial externalities of city life) can compensate for the loss of space in our living arrangements.

[49]   *The difference elaborated*
Neo-Malthusians would enlarge the concept of territories and suggest that broad territories are characterized by access to the natural environment, good jobs and houses with gardens. Territories set an upper limit on population size of a society so that if broad territories were made mandatory then population size would be smaller. This is because the resource requirements would mean that couples could not afford large families. Welfare economists think that if people wish to live in narrow territories with the collective consequence of large population size then priority should be given to raising prosperity to compensate for any adverse external effects.

[50]   *Concluding arguments*
Here then, is the nub of the matter. Most welfare economists think that in the long run it is the desires and aspirations of people that matter. The way to satisfy these is with prosperity which enables people to exercise their choices better. Both efficiency and technical progress are conducive to prosperity. Moreover, they can be 'good' for the environment (although our history does not confirm this). Hence population problems are relatively unimportant since prosperity can compensate for or 'cure' such problems. Consequently, the optimum population size can be very large. So the challenge to human ingenuity is to raise and spread prosperity without damaging the environment further. The neo-Malthusians think that population problems are extremely serious and arise from the unintended collective consequences of people's desires and aspirations. Since the society's optimum population size is thought to be small, people must be made to want the implied small family size by using information, argument and incentives. In this way individual aspirations can be made to reconcile with the optimal collective outcome. If it turns out that world inequality is likely to persist and environmental constraints on prosperity will tighten then the argument for the above neo-Malthusian preventive measure has added force. So, the challenge to human ingenuity is to get people to want to live in broad territories with our existing resources at hand. They should want to because they would be better off.

12.3 Major changes and recurrent themes

Several themes recur throughout this monograph, against a backdrop which spans major changes in our history. These profoundly influential changes can be traced to our capability to exploit the natural environment for material prosperity. Changes that are particularly relevant for the subject of population analysis are: (1) unprecedented access to resources, (2) changes in survival uncertainty, (3) health changes, particularly falling mortality and rising longevity, (4) taste changes induced by artefacts that serve as substitutes for our genetic urge to hereditary immortality. Such changes have influenced household fertility decisions and thereby the collective consequences of such private decisions.

One recurring theme has been a comparison of ecological and economic thinking. Both analyses rest on resource constraint and given preferences. A significant difference between the two lies in the specification of preferences.

i) Preferences: genes versus memes

The distinction between genes (our biological urges) and memes (our creative urges) is profound. Memes have to do with our brains. We humans have the capacity for abstract thought and can develop artefacts of beauty, knowledge, and so on. Call this non-biological artefact memes, genes being essentially biological.

Some scientists believe that the biological evolution of humans has run its course and that cultural evolution has taken over (see Fletcher, 1974). Cultural activities require a powerful brain and in this respect no life form comes near to us humans. Over the years, the greatest growth has been in the temperate lobes of our frontal brain controlling speech and abstract thought so that we, unlike other animal species, have a new dimension; we can think about the future. We can plan, have aims and purposes. As a result, we also have traditions and have accumulated knowledge over successive generations. We are unique in that information can be passed on, not only by genes but also by word of mouth, by books and by other technological aids.

The power of the distinction between genes and memes for population analysis lies in the fact that memes are a substitute for children, the latter being a manifestation of our biological urge for hereditary immortality. Potentially, our brains can override our genes although it is very difficult to say what urge drives a person at any given time. The picture of us could well be that some of us are largely driven by genes, some by memes and some by a conflict of the two; some of us have not become independent of our biological origins, some are totally free and some are in the process of becoming free. (See Gellner, 1989). The fact that people are heterogeneous also complicates matters for in between genes and memes there are urges related to happiness, self-indulgence and power.

ii) Decision making: uncertainty and gambles

Family size decisions are made in an environment of uncertainty. There is the uncertainty concerning child mortality and uncertainty of economic survival. If a couple is not sure which of its children will survive then family size planning is somewhat of a gamble. Such gambles were taken in the past and, to a certain extent, are still being taken today. However, presently there is considerable uncertainty concerning the economic success of children when they become adults and parents attempt to bias this gamble in their children's favour by endowing them with human capital. In the instance where parental resources are not meagre, as in the first world, the higher cost of equipping a less able child with human capital can often be met. However, where parental resources are meagre, as in the third world, allocation of parental capital to children of differing ability is a more complicated gamble.

iii) Technical progress and resource constraint

Ecologists think that genes and resources drive population size. Our unique ability to exploit the environment and thereby change niches at will has given us access to a vast supply of material resources. Ecologists think that the urge to hereditary immortality is so strong that a couple uses up all its resources to support as many children as it can, regardless of any collective consequences. Incidentally, it is a fact that technical progress together with our adaptability has enabled us to support a staggering number of 5.8 billion human lives today.

iv) Collective consequences of private decisions

Ecologists think that there is an optimum population size so that once population grows beyond its optimum size, adverse external effects dominate. The population problem then, in fact, becomes a scale problem since the greater the population size, the bigger the external effects. If the population size does exceed the optimum size then the situation can be likened to the famous 'tragedy of the commons' (Hardin, 1968; Muhsam, 1973). As in the 'commons' example, there are welfare gains to be made if numbers are kept down. These gains are the fruits of technology which imply a higher material standard of living as well as more space, less environmental damage and hence greater survival chances. However, in practice, as it happens in the 'commons' parable, all the rents get dissipated.

Ecologists do not deny that human beings have choice and can also deliberate on matters such as the optimum population size which animals cannot. However, they contend that when it comes to individual choice concerning fertility there is a powerful genetic influence. On the other hand, we can make use of our ability to formulate conscious thoughts to deliberate about the collective consequences of individual fertility decisions.

Economists think that individual fertility decisions are largely governed by rational thought. Population problems result when rational individuals face the 'wrong' economic signals. However, individuals can consciously weigh up whether they can be adequately compensated for reducing fertility by an increase in material prosperity. Thus the solution to any collective problem arising from individual fertility decisions is either to provide the 'right' economic signals or raise overall material prosperity.

v)   Comparing ecologists and economists

Ecologists think that the solution to the 'overpopulation' problem is to disconnect technical progress from population, that is, to reap the fruits of technical progress by persuading people to live in broad territories instead of more being packed into narrow niche-spaces. Economists think that there is no causality running from technical progress to population size so that the policy of disconnection does not arise.

Another way of bringing out the difference between the two schools is by using the concept of terms of trade: the rate at which material goods can be substituted for children. Ecologists are persuaded that it is very expensive to compensate couples for agreeing to have smaller families; indeed it may be impossible if people have lexicographic preferences. Economists, on the other hand, believe that you can compensate. Notwithstanding this disagreement, it seems that terms of trade vary across cultures and also over time. It may also be the case that they vary across wealth holdings and income levels. Since there is a problem of asymmetric information concerning a given couple's preferences, we really have little idea about the magnitude of the terms of trade.

vi)   Institutions

According to ecologists, we have the following choice: we can use our resources to support a large population at subsistence level or we can use the resources to raise the standard of living of a smaller population. In order to accomplish the latter, ecologists advocate the institutional device of a territory. They think that at present we still live like territorial species but have neglected the spatial dimension to our territories, a vivid example of this being that of slums in third world cities. Since the number of territories determines population size we can use the resources generated by technical progress to increase the quality and size of our territories which would mean fewer territories and therefore a smaller population.

Economists think that the price mechanism may be giving inaccurate signals about the cost of having a child. If so, then overcrowding results which serves as a surrogate price to raise the child cost. But by the time that overcrowding has had a chance to influence decisions at household level, we may already have arrived at the collective outcome of overpopulation. (This comes as no surprise to ecologists who think that given the strong private incentive to procreate and the inaccurate value placed on resources to support children, resources are bound to be used up to support more and more people in narrow niche-spaces.) So, according to economists, the solution is to ensure the smooth working of the market institution. Economists also think that our powerful brains are capable of both overriding our genetic urges and devising institutions to compensate for any overcrowding. They point to the tremendous improvements in the material standard of living in the West and the city life of New York, Paris and London as evidence of compensation for overcrowding. Economists believe that technical progress will 'release' the extra resources from the world's environment. The underlying assumption is that the resource cake is so large that there is enough for everyone's prosperity. It remains, simply to 'get at' the huge uneaten cake.

vii) The future – if nothing is done

According to ecologists, in the medium term (25 to 50 years), the majority will live in shrinking territories and in misery and poverty if nothing is done to control population. Indeed, UNFPA, 1995 predicts that there will be a continuing shift of rural populations to urban areas with 56 per cent of the global population expected to live in urban areas by 2015. (This means that the urban population is expected to grow from 2.6 billion to 4 billion in just 20 years.) The most rapid urbanization is expected to be in developing countries where the lives of people in existing slums are pathetic.

According to economists, in the medium term, competition should ensue if nothing is done. This can have a double effect on population. One effect of competition is price changes which should raise the cost of child rearing (an increase in higher education fees, an increase in price of firewood). Another effect is a possible increase in resources. Consider global competition.

We noted in Chapter 3 that in our history the institution of the market has contributed to increases in resources. Markets do that by facilitating specialization. This point was made in the context of city-states and many commentators have argued that recently a similar phenomenon is occurring on the global stage. Several significant changes over the last couple of decades have given impetus to global competition, among them (1) the collapse of central economic planning such as that in the former Soviet Union; (2) the adoption of market discipline by the population giants of China and India; (3) the liberalization of money markets where, in 1995, 1 trillion dollars were estimated to have been traded daily; (4) the revolution in communications which has made markets more accessible; (5) the ease of technological transfer which has meant that production can be carried out in many more locations.

The optimists argue that global competition will result in greater prosperity as it will compel countries to specialize. However, that may make some populations vulnerable. Consider the case of Rwanda. Some years ago the country shifted to producing cash crops for export and incomes rose, financing the imports of food. Then civil war ensued and imports dwindled. There resulted a shortage of food and many, especially children, were left undernourished. The point is this: ecologists think that global competition simply postpones a Malthusian crisis and that when it does occur it will be on a bigger scale.

12.4   Final word

With the combination of human ingenuity, human adaptability and greater technical progress, we have seen a tremendous transformation of the natural landscape accompanied by phenomenal population growth. The majority of observers think that the quality and the quantity of our environmental capital has significantly decreased. Against that, human artefacts have increased and since prosperity is measured in terms of artefacts, the standard of material living, for developed nations at least, has risen. However, we appear to have persistent inequality and the number of undernourished humans is on the increase; it is thought that currently one-sixth of the world's population, about one billion, is persistently undernourished. Many people also believe that a worsening of mental health in the West has been a heavy price to pay for its material prosperity.

As predicted by the ecological model, the population growth curve of most developed nations has traced out the sigmoid curve. The flattening out of the curve (that is, fertility decline) is attributed to 'environmental limits' inducing an increase in child-rearing costs. However, according to economists there are other factors at work, such as a taste change induced by prosperity. This causes our brains to override our genetic propensity to breed. Of course the ecological model also predicts sigmoid curves for third world populations so that currently many such countries can be thought of as being on the steep segment of the curve. By the time the curves flatten out, world population could well be 12 to 15 billion.

Neo-Malthusians think that the external effects of population size are considerable and usually adverse so that we should actively aim for the smaller optimum size. In other words, neo-Malthusians believe in preventing the occurrence of external effects and so prescribe immediate intervention. The advocated intervention largely aims at raising the cost of child rearing.

Economists think that population size does not matter because people can be materially compensated for the adverse external effects. As opposed to the preventive stance of the neo-Malthusians, economists prescribe greater prosperity as a cure for any adverse external effects associated with population size. There are three problems with this stance. The first, noted by ecologists, is that the point may have been reached where the damage done to the resilience of the natural environment is irreversible. The second is our poor record in devising institutional arrangements, such as territoriality, so as to live better.

Animals in nature do follow a sigmoid population growth curve but their territorial arrangements mean that the final population size is smaller than what it otherwise would be. The third is persistent inequality. To enable the rich of the world to indulge in their lifestyles and to maintain or increase their consumption persistent inequality and mass suffering look like being necessary. After all, the affluent do need a massive resource and environmental support and that may imply that the usual trade-off between prosperity and the environment is denied to the poor countries.

The most telling of the above three problems is the environmental constraint. This reduces our set of choices. Prosperity for all then must mean a smaller world population. To accomplish that, people must desire smaller families. To this end, human capital led development instantly raises cost of child rearing, thereby inducing people to want smaller families. It is hoped that human capital also equips us better to meet the challenge of prosperity without damaging the environment further. We have no idea how to finance such development and there is no certainty that human capital will do the trick. But it is the most humane option that we have.

References

Andrewartha, H.G. and Birch, L.C. (1954), *The Distribution and Abundance of Animals*, Chicago: University of Chicago Press.

Apter, M. (1992), *The Dangerous Edge*, Free Press.

Ardrey, R. (1967), *The Territorial Imperative*, London: Collins.

Ardrey, R. (1970), *The Social Contract*, New York: Atheneum.

Axelrod, R. (1984), *The Evolution of Cooperation*, New York: Basic Books.

Axelrod, R. (1987), 'Laws of Life', *The Sciences*, **27**, pp. 44–51.

Barro, R. (1974), 'Are Government Bonds Net Wealth?', *Journal of Political Economy*, **82**, pp. 1095–117.

Basu, A. (1992), *Culture, the Status of Women and Demographic Behaviour*, Oxford.

Bateson, P.P.G. (1988), 'The Active Role of Behaviour in Evolution', in M.W. Howard and S.W. Fox, (eds.), *Evolutionary Processes and Metaphors*, New York: John Wiley.

Becker, G.S. (1974), 'A Theory of Social Interactions', *Journal of Political Economy*, **82**, pp. 1063–93.

Becker, G.S. (1981), *A Treatise on the Family*, (Cambridge, Mass.).

Becker, G.S. and H.G. Lewis (1973), 'Interaction between Quality and Quantity of Children', *Journal of Political Economy*.

Becker, G.S. and Tomes, N. (1976), 'Child Endowments and the Quantity and Quality of Children', *Journal of Political Economy*, **84**, pp. S142–S63.

Bengtsson, T. (1992), 'Lessons from the Past: the Demographic Transition Revised', *Ambio*, **21**.

Berryman, A. (1981), *Population Systems*, New York: Plenum Publishing Corp.

Birdsall, N. (1988), 'Economic Approaches to Population Growth' in H. Chenery and T.N. Srinivasan (eds), *Handbook of Development Economics*, Amsterdam: North Holland, pp. 477–542.

Birdsall, N. and C.C. Griffin (1988), 'Fertility and Poverty in Developing Countries', *Journal of Policy Modelling*, **10**, pp. 29–56.

Birdsall, N. and R. Sabot (1993), 'Virtuous Circles: Human Capital, Growth and Equity in East Asia', World Bank, Policy Research Department.

Bledsoe, C. (1994), 'Children are Like Young Bamboo Trees: Potentiality and Reproduction in Sub-Saharan Africa', in K. Lindahl-Kiessling and H. Landberg (eds), *Population, Economic Development, and the Environment*, Oxford: Oxford University Press, pp. 105–38.

161

Boulding, K.E. (1964), *The Meaning of the Twentieth Century*, New York: Harper and Row.

Boulding, K.E. (1977), 'Commons and Community: The Idea of a Public', in G. Hardin and J. Baden (eds), Managing the Commons, San Francisco: W.H. Freeman and Co.

Boyd, R. and Richerson, P. (1985), *Culture and the Evolutionary Process*, Chicago: University of Chicago Press.

Brown, L.R., W. Chandler, C. Flavin, J. Jacobson, C. Pollock, S. Postel, L. Starke and E. Wolf (1987), *State of the World*, New York: Norton.

Cain, M. (1977), 'The Economic Activities of Children in a Village in Bangladesh', *Population and Development Review*, **3**, pp. 201–27.

Caldwell, J.C. (1976) 'Toward a Restatement of Demographic Transition Theory', *Population and Development Review*, **2**, pp. 321–66.

Caldwell, J.C. (1977a), 'The Economic Rationality of High Fertility: An Investigation Illustrated with Nigerian Data', *Population Studies*, **31**.

Caldwell, J.C. (1977b), *The Persistence of High Fertility: Population Prospects in the Third World*, Canberra: Australian National University Press.

Caldwell, J.C. (1981), 'The Mechanisms of Demographic Change in Historical Perspective', *Population Studies*, **35**.

Caldwell, J.C. (1982), *Theory of Fertility Decline*, New York: Academic Press.

Chesnais, Jean-Claude (1992), *The Demographic Transition*, Oxford: Clarendon Press.

Chudacoff, H.P (1975), *The Evolution of American Urban Society*, Englewood Cliffs: Prentice-Hall.

Cigno, A. (1994), *Economics of the Family*, Oxford: Clarendon Press.

Cipolla, C.M. (1963), *The Economic History of World Population*, New York: Smith.

Cohen, M.N. (1977), *The Food Crisis in Prehistory: Overpopulation and the Origins of Agriculture*, New Haven: Yale University Press.

Colinvaux, P.A. (1975), 'An Ecologist's View of History', *Yale Review*, **64**, pp. 357–69.

Colinvaux, P.A. (1976), 'The Human Breeding Strategy', *Nature*, **261**, pp. 356–7.

Colinvaux, P.A. (1978), *Why Big Fierce Animals are Rare*, Princeton: Princeton University Press.

Colinvaux, P.A. (1980), *The Fate of Nations*, New York: Simon and Schuster.

Cosmides, L. and J. Tooby (1989), 'Evolutionary Psychology and the Generation of Culture' (part 2), *Ethology and Sociobiology*, **10**, pp. 51–97.

Cotts Watkins, S. (1990) 'From Local to National Communities: The Transformation of Demographic Regions in Western Europe 1870–1960', *Population and Development Review*, **16**.

Crosson, P. and J.R. Anderson (1991), 'Resources and Global Food Prospects: Supply and Demand for Cereals to 2030', World Bank, Technical Paper No. 184.

CSE (1990), *Human-Nature Interactions in a Central Himalayan Village: A Case Study of Village Bemru*, New Delhi.

Dahlberg, F. (1981), *Woman the Gatherer*, New Haven: Yale University Press.

Daly, H.E. (1974), 'The Economics of the Steady State', *American Economic Review*.

Daly, H.E. (1982), 'Chicago School Individualism Versus Sexual Reproduction: A Critique of Becker and Tomes', *Journal of Economic Issues*.

Daly, H.E. and J.E. Cobb Jr. (1990), *For the Common Good*, London: Green Print.

Dasgupta, P. (1992), 'Population, Resources and Poverty', *Ambio*, **21**.

Dasgupta, P. (1993), *An Inquiry into Well-Being and Destitution*, Oxford: Clarendon Press.

Dawkins, R. (1989), *The Selfish Gene*, New York: Oxford University Press.

Desai, M.J. and A.R. Shah (1983), 'Bequest and Inheritance in Nuclear Families and Joint Families', *Economica*, **50**, pp. 193–202.

Dooley, M.D. (1982) 'Labour Supply and Fertility of Married Women: An Analysis with Grouped and Ungrouped Data from the 1970 U.S. Census', *Journal of Human Resources*, **17**, pp. 499–532.

Douglas, R. (1991)'The Commons and Property Rights: towards a Synthesis of Demography and Ecology', in R.V. Andelson (ed.), *Commons Without Tragedy*, pp. 1–26.

Durham, W. (1991), *Coevolution*, Palo Alto: Stanford University Press.

Easterlin, R.A., A.A. Pollak and M.L. Wachter (1980), 'Toward a More General Model of Fertility Determination: Endogenous Preferences and Natural Fertility', in R.A. Easterlin (ed.), *Population and Economic Change in Developing Countries*, Chicago: University of Chicago Press.

Ehrlich, P.R. and A.E. Ehrlich (1992), 'The Value of Biodiversity', Ambio, **21**.

Elton, C.S. (1927), *Animal Ecology*, New York: Macmillan Press, p. 29.

Elvin, M. (1973), *The Pattern of the Chinese Past*, Stanford: Stanford University Press.

Fleisher, B.M. and G.F. Rhodes (1979), 'Fertility, Women's Wage Rates, and Labor Supply', *American Economic Review*, **69**(1), pp. 14–24.

Fletcher, W.W. (1974), *Modern Man looks at Evolution*, Redhill: Fontana.

Flink, J.J. (1975), *The Car Culture*, Cambridge: MIT Press.

Fogel, R. (1994) 'The Relevance of Malthus for the Study of Mortality Today: Long-Run Influences on Health, Mortality, Labour Force Participation, and Population Growth', in K. Lindahl-Kiessling and H. Landberg (eds), *Population, Economic Development, and the Environment*, Oxford: Oxford University Press, pp. 231–84.

Foley, R. (1987), *Another Unique Species: Patterns in Human Evolutionary Ecology*, Harlow: Longman.

Fotey, R. (1995), *Humans before Humanity*, Oxford: Blackwell.

Gamble, C. (1994), *Timewalkers: The Prehistory of Global Colonization*, Stroud: Alan Sutton.

Gellner, E. (1989), 'Culture, Constraint and Community: Semantic and Coercive Compensations for the Under-determination of Homo Sapiens' in P.A. Mellars, and C.B. Stringer (eds), *The Human Revolution: Behavioural and Biological Perspectives on the Origins of Modern Humans*, Edinburgh: Edinburgh University Press, pp. 514–28.

George, H. (1962), *Progress and Poverty*, New York: Robert Schalkenbach Foundation.

George, S. (1977), *How the Other Half Dies: The Real Reasons for World Hunger*, Montclair: Allanheld, Osmun and Co.

Gergen, K.J., M.S. Greenberg and R.H. Willis, (eds) (1980), *Social Exchange: Advances in Theory and Research*, New York: Plenum Press.

Goodman, D. (1975), 'The Theory of Diversity and Stability in Ecology', *Quarterly Review of Biology*, **50**, pp. 237–66.

Halpern, D. (1995), *Mental Health and Built Environment*, Taylor & Francis.

Hardin, G. (1968), 'The Tragedy of the Commons', *Science*, **162**, pp. 1243–8.

Heer, D.M. (1975), 'Marketable Licences for Babies: Boulding's Proposal Revisited', *Social Biology*, Spring.

Hendrick, P. (1984), *Population Biology: The Evolution and Ecology of Populations*, Boston: Jones & Barlett Publishers.

Hetaserani, S. and J. Roumasset (1992), 'Institutional Change and Demographic Transition in Rural Thailand', *Economic Development and Cultural Change*, **39**.

Hill, K. (1992), 'Fertility and Mortality Trends in the Developing World', *Ambio*, **21**.

Hohenberg, P.M. and L.H. Lees, (1985), *The Making of Urban Europe 1000–1950*, Cambridge: Harvard University Press.

Holling, C.S. (1973), 'Resilience and Stability of Ecological System', *Annual Review of Ecology and Systematics*, **4**, pp. 1–23.

Holling, C.S., D.W. Schindler, B.W. Walker and J. Rooghgarden, (1994), 'Biodiversity in the Functioning of Ecosystems: An Ecological Primer and Synthesis', in Perrings *et al* (eds), *Biodiversity Loss: Ecological and Economic Issues*, Cambridge.

Klopfer, P.H. (1969), *Habitats and Territories*, New York: Basic Books

Krebs, C.K. (1988), *The Message of Ecology*, New York: Harper and Row.

Krupat, E. (1985), *People in Cities*, Cambridge: Cambridge University Press.

Lee, R.B. and I. De Vore, (1968), *Man the Hunter*, Chicago: Chicago University Press.

Lewis, R. (1960), *The Evolution Man*, Harmondsworth: Penguin.

Lovejoy, C.O. (1981), 'The Origin of Man', *Science*, **211**, pp. 341–50.

Lynch, K. (1960), *The Image of the City*, Cambridge: MIT Press.

Malthus, T.R. (1798), *An Essay on the Principle of Population*, Harmondsworth: Penguin, 1970.

May, D.A. and D.M. Heer, (1968), 'Son Survivorship Motivation and Family Size in India: A Computer Simulation', *Population Studies*, **22**.

McEvedy, C. and R. Jones, (1979), *Atlas of World Population History*, Princeton: Princeton University Press.

McGuire, J. and B.M. Popkin, (1989), 'Beating the Zero-Sum Game: Women and Nutrition in the Third World: Part 1, *Food and Nutrition Bulletin*, **11**.

McKeown, T. (1976), *The Modern Rise of Population*, New York.

McKeown, T. (1978), 'Fertility, Mortality and Cause of Death: An Examination of Issues Related to the Modern Rise of Population', *Population Studies*, **32**, pp. 535–42.

Mellars, P.A. and C.B. Stringer, (eds) (1989), *The Human Revolution: Behavioural and Biological Perspectives on the Origins of Modern Humans*, Edinburgh: Edinburgh University Press.

Mincer, J. (1963), 'Market Prices, Opportunity Costs and Income Effects', in C. Christ *et al* (eds), *Measurement in Economics*, pp. 75–9, Stanford, California: Stanford University Press.

Mitchell, D.C. and M.D. Ingco (1993), 'The World Food Outlook', World Bank, Washington D.C., International Economics Department, November.

Moffitt, R. (1984), 'The Estimation of Fertility Equations on Panel Data', *Journal of Human Resources*, **19**(1), pp. 22–34.

Morris, D. (1994), *The Human Animal*, London: BBC Books.

Muhsam, H.V. (1973), 'A World Population Policy for the World Population Year', *Journal of Peace Research*, 1–2, pp. 97–9.

Newman, S.P. and S. Lonsdale, (1996), *Human Jungle*, London: Ebury Press.

Norman, D.A. (1988), *The Psychology of Everyday Things*, Basic Books.

Nugent, J. and T. Gillaspy (1983), 'Old Age Pension and Fertility in Rural Areas of Less Developed Countries: Some Evidence from Mexico', *Economic Development and Cultural Change*, **31**.

Oshima, H. (1992), 'Impact of Economic Development on Labour Markets, Education, and Population in Asia', *Ambio* **21**.

Pack, H. and J. Page (1993), 'Accumulation, Exports, and Growth in the High Performing Asian Economies', paper presented at the Carnegie Rochester Conference on Public Policy, April.

Passmore, J. (1974), *Man's Responsibility for Nature: Ecological Problems and Western Traditions*, New York: Scribner.

Pearl, R. (1927), 'The Growth of Populations', *Quarterly Review of Biology*, **2**, pp. 532–48.

Perrings, C., K.G. Mâler, C. Folke, C.S. Holling and B.O. Jonsson (eds) (1994), *Biodiversity Loss: Ecological and Economic Issues*, Cambridge.

Perusse, D. (1993), 'Cultural and Reproductive Success in Industrial Societies: Testing the Relationship at the Proximate and Ultimate Levels', *Behavioural and Brain Sciences*, **16**, pp. 267–322.

Polanyi, K. (1980), *The Great Transformation*, New York: Octagon.

Rapoport, A. (1960), *Fights, Games and Debates*, Ann Arbor: University of Michigan Press.

Rosenzweig, M.R. and T.P. Schultz (1985), 'The Demand for and Supply of Births: Fertility and its Life-Cycle Consequences', *American Economic Review*, **75**, pp. 992–1015.

Rosenzweig, M.R. and K. Wolpin, (1980), 'Testing the Quantity–Quality Fertility Model: the Use of Twins as a Natural Experiment', *Econoamerica*, **48**, pp. 227–40.

Samuelson, P.A. (1958), 'An Exact Consumption Loan Model of Interest with or without the Social Contrivance of Money', *Journal of Political Economy*, **66**, pp. 923–33.

Sen, A.K. (1994), 'Population and Reasoned Agency', in K. Lindahl-Kiessling and H. Landberg (eds), *Population, Economic Development, and the Environment*, Oxford: Oxford University Press, pp. 51–78.

Simon, J. (1981), *The Ultimate Resource*, Princeton.

Simon, J. (ed) (1996), *The State of Humanity*, Oxford: Blackwell.

Simon, J.L. and H. Kahn (1984), *The Resourceful Earth: A Response to Global 2000*, Oxford.

Sjoberg, G. (1960), *The Preindustrial City*, New York: Free Press.

Sutcliffe, A. (ed.) (1984), *Metropolis 1890–1940*, London: Mansell.

Thomas, K. (1983), *Man and the Natural World: A History of the Modern Sensibility*, New York: Pantheon.

Thurow, L.C. (1994), 'New Game, New Rules, New Strategies', *RSA Journal*, November, pp. 50–56.

Todaro, M.P. (1989), *Economic Development in the Third World*, New York: Longman.

Trivers, R. (1971), 'The Evolution of Reciprocal Altruism', *Quarterly Review of Biology*, **46**, pp. 35–56.

Ucko, P.J. and Dimbleby, G.W. (1969), *The Domestication and Exploitation of Plants and Animals*, Chicago: Aldine.

United Nations (1953), *The Determinants and Consequences of Population Trends, Population Studies No. 17*, New York.

United Nations (1973), *The Determinants and Consequences of Populaton Trends, Population Studies No. 50*, New York.

Wattenberg, B. and H. Zinsmeister, (1986), 'The Birth Dearth: The Geopolitical Consequences', *Public Opinion*, December/January.

Whyte, W. (1988), *Rediscovering the Centre*, Anchor Books.

Willis, R.J. (1973), 'A New Approach to the Economic Theory of Fertility Behaviour', *Journal of Political Economy*, Supplement, pp. 514–64.

Willis, R.J. (1987), 'Externalities and Population' in D.G. Johnson and R.D. Lee (eds), *Population Growth and Economic Development: Issues and Evidence*, Madison, Wis., pp. 661–702.

Willis, R.J. (1994), 'Economic Analysis of Fertility: Micro Foundations and Aggregate Implications', in K. Lindahl-Kiessling and H. Landberg (eds), *Population, Economic Development, and the Environment*, Oxford: Oxford University Press, pp. 139–71.

Wilson, E.O. (1992), *The Diversity of Life*, New York.

World Bank (1984), *World Development Report: Population Change and Economic Development*, Oxford: World Bank.

World Bank (1991), *The Population, Agriculture and Environmental Nexus in Sub-Saharan Africa*, Washington, DC: World Bank.

World Bank (1993), *The East Asian Miracle*, Oxford: World Bank.

Wrigley, E.A. and R.S. Schofield (1981), *The Population History of England 1541–1871: A Reconstruction*, London.

Index

Africa
  contraceptive use in 68, 127
  food supply problems in 79
  population trends in 63, 64, 65, 67–8
  prosperity strategy for 128–30
agriculture
  development of 1, 24–5, 29, 113
  future food production 78–80
aid programmes 129
Anderson, J. R. 80
Andrewartha, H. G. 23
animal herding, development of 24
Apter, M. 137
Ardrey, R. 12, 99
Axelrod, R. 103

Bangladesh 65, 69, 121
Barro, R. 61
Bateson, P. P. G. 12
Becker, G. S. 55, 59, 61
behavioural ecology 4, 19
  family size decisions and 13–17,
    112–13
  Malthus and 39–40, 48
Bengtsson, T. 110
Berryman, A. 78
Birch, L. C. 23
Birdsall, N. 125, 127
birth control programmes, government
    120–24, 151
birth permits 123–4, 151
Black Death 38, 40
Bledsoe, C. 67–8
Boulding, K. E. 30, 41, 106, 123, 146
Boyd, R. 16
Brazil 105, 114–15, 116, 119
Britain 38–9, 110, 111, 141
Brown, L. R. 72

Cain, M. 69
Caldwell, J. C. 70
Caldwell Hypothesis 70–71
Canada 93

capital market reform 113, 150
car ownership 141
caste system 28
Centre for Science and the Environment
    (CSE) 69, 85
certificate escalation 127–8
Chesnais, J.-C. 44
Chicago model of demographic
    transition 50–62
  changes in costs of goods/services in
    59–60
  changes in wife's wage in 57–9
  child and adult services in 50–51
  comparative statics analysis of 55–7
  costs in 51–2
  preferences in 52–5
China 7, 28, 29, 75, 79, 120, 122–3, 128,
    142, 151
Chudacoff, H. P. 141
Cigno, A. 55
Cipolla, C. M. 38
cities 135–43, 146, 152
  adaptation to life in 137–8
  benefits of 138–9, 152
  crime and violence in 136–7
  development of 26, 111, 135–7
  future of 7, 141–2, 143
  overcrowding and 111, 140
  Third World 139–40, 143, 152
  unplanned growth of 140–41
co-operation 99
  breakdown of 105–6
  development of 12, 100, 104–5
  game theory and 100–105, 107–8
Cobb, J. E. 45
Cohen, M. N. 25
Colinvaux, P. A. 14, 17, 28
collective action 99
common property 95, 98, 155
community action 99
consumer goods, children viewed as 40,
    46
contraception 16, 68, 126–7

169